Books of Merit

MYSTIC TRUDEAU

BY B.W. POWE

BOOKS

A Climate Charged
The Solitary Outlaw
A Tremendous Canada of Light
Outage
The Unsaid Passing
Towards a Canada of Light
Mystic Trudeau
These Shadows Remain

EDITOR

Light Onwords/Light Onwards—
The Living Literacies Record

CD-ROM

"Noise of Time," in *The Glenn Gould Profile*

EVENTS (Program Coordinator)

Marshall McLuhan: What If He Was Right?,
York University, 1997

The Trudeau Era, York University, 1998

Living Literacies, York University, 2002

MYSTIC TRUDEAU

THE FIRE AND THE ROSE

—|—

B.W. POWE

Thomas Allen Publishers
Toronto

Copyright © 2007 by B.W. Powe

All rights reserved. No part of this work may be reproduced or
transmitted in any form or by any means—graphic, electronic, or
mechanical, including photocopying, recording, taping, or information
storage and retrieval systems—without the prior written permission
of the publisher, or in the case of photocopying or other reprographic
copying, a licence from the Canadian Copyright Licensing Agency

Library and Archives Canada Cataloguing in Publication

Powe, B. W. (Bruce W.), 1955–
Mystic Trudeau : the fire and the rose / B.W. Powe.

ISBN 978-0-88762-281-6

1. Trudeau, Pierre Elliott, 1919–2000.
2. Trudeau, Pierre Elliott, 1919–2000—Philosophy.
3. Trudeau, Pierre Elliott, 1919–2000—Influence.
4. Trudeau, Pierre Elliott, 1919–2000—Political and social views.
5. National characteristics, Canadian.
6. Prime ministers—Canada—Biography.   I. Title.

FC626.T7P69   2007   971.064'4092   C2007-904402-6

Editor: Patrick Crean
Jacket image: Jean-Marc Carisse/www.carisse.org

Published by Thomas Allen Publishers,
a division of Thomas Allen & Son Limited,
145 Front Street East, Suite 209,
Toronto, Ontario M5A 1E3 Canada

www.thomas-allen.com

The publisher gratefully acknowledges the support of
The Ontario Arts Council for its publishing program.
The Ontario Arts Council is an agency of the Government of Ontario.

We acknowledge the support of the Canada Council for the Arts, which last
year invested $20.1 million in writing and publishing throughout Canada.

We acknowledge the Government of Ontario through the
Ontario Media Development Corporation's Ontario Book Initiative.

We acknowledge the financial support of the Government of
Canada through the Book Publishing Industry Development
Program (BPIDP) for our publishing activities.

11 10 09 08 07   1 2 3 4 5

Ancient forest friendly: printed on 100% post-consumer recycled paper

Printed and bound in Canada

*For Alys Maude Powe
who has watched over
the coming and going
of so many books*

Every human being cries out silently to be read differently.
SIMONE WEIL

There is more in a human life than our theories of it allow.
JAMES HILLMAN

"To intercalate realities" writes Balthazar "is the only way to be faithful to Time, for at every moment in Time the possibilities are endless in their multiplicity. Life consists in the act of choice. The perpetual reservations of judgment and the perpetual choosing."
LAWRENCE DURRELL

Politics, like the climate, is a non-linear system.
AL GORE

CONTENTS

I

Emanations, Destinies

1

II

Patterns, Seeds, Cloaking, Soul Circling

69

III

Forms, Eulogies, Images and Symbols

125

IV

Substance, Pressures, Beyond, Pulse in Matter

201

Notes and Acknowledgments

265

MYSTIC TRUDEAU

I

EMANATIONS, DESTINIES

The soul is the human being considered
as having a value in itself.

SIMONE WEIL

The arc of the moral universe is indeed long
but it does bend toward justice.

CORMAC MCCARTHY

. . . a completely liberal world, the world
of the free movement of the spirit.

NORTHROP FRYE

How nicely I burn.

ARTHUR RIMBAUD

Pierre, once more: this is unfinished business. Old friend, here is another reflection on you before you recede into fragments of memory and fading archival footage. Pierre, again, because there is more to say about you, especially to those who may be starting to forget your visionary pride. Your uncanny unfolding won't rest. Ghostlike you visit, posing unanswered questions. You are still sounding on deep vibrating frequencies.

You were Prime Minister of Canada a generation ago (1968 to 1978, then 1980 to 1984). My children don't know what you did, and what you advocated. Their friends attend a school named after you, and yet they can't answer the question, Who was he? Students, young people, sometimes muse on you, but see you disappearing into their elders' hearsay.

We watch you transforming into a persistent media spirit that often beckons from screens and images. But what were you saying? Why do I need to summon you again?

"Don't bend your knees before anyone," you wrote in your diary in 1940. "Keep your head high before the powerful." You courted audacity for yourself, and for your country. Obtrusive and evasive in your personality, a presence at once clear and obscured, you invited spiritual fire into you. "Let's batter down the totems, let's break the taboos," you said in 1950, in *Cité libre*. Light and mystery—intensities and vision—come with the fire; and with it comes ashes, the roughness of the char. Actors on the global stage may burn brightly, and sometimes flame out into pieces.

Pierre, we are still dealing with your complexities.

"Reason over passion," you said, directing our attention towards the Platonic *noûs*, or Universal Spirit. Hence reason, in your articulation, was an expression of the soul's aspirations; it was the calm of transcendental intention. Passion was animal flesh, raw desire gnawing and ripping at its earthly limitations. These passions were to be feared only if undirected by the conscience of the higher self. Mind was the key to the process of enlightenment. Hence reason was the first principle, light itself.

You said you were a political pragmatist (and so you were), and yet you eased into inspired speech, in 1970, when you spoke of "the threefold gift of transcendence, individual worth, and justice."

But Pierre, this is the time of assassins and terror. We are poised "on the naked edge of knives" (Pablo Neruda). There are wars that have no end in sight. Last calls resound like the tolling of bells. Hard, closed-off political leaders won't weep for their children, and steep themselves in the agendas of fear. They try to prohibit the images of the sacrifices they demand. There are battle-cries declared on behalf of duty. You would never have wept in public either, but you would have asked us, Where do you want this country to go?

I remember you because at a point lost to us the idea of a vast cosmopolitan Canada uprooted you. "I'm a nomad by inclination, but also by necessity," you said in a 1948 letter to your younger brother, Charles. You tore yourself away from the cage of categories. In 1961, in what must have been your manifesto, again in *Cité Libre*, you wrote, "Open up the borders, our people are suffocating to death." Did you know that when you came to the idea of the opening (or this came to you) that it would demand a deepening of the self? It was an epiphany, a crack, a lifting, a widening. Your heart and mind somehow broke to let in the new.

There was the idea of the cosmopolis, the electrified global city and the heated nearness of souls. This is the pluralist society, rootless and free from blood-ties and narrow nationalisms. "The role of leadership today is to encourage the embrace of a global ethic," you said in 1975.

Then there was "the just society," your ambiguous tag phrase. "Justice to me is a warm spirit, born of tolerance and wisdom, present everywhere," you said in 1972. After you uttered such words, you may have been astonished by them. No one is sure where you discovered the phrase. Who gave it to you? Was it your friend, the philosopher and poet F.R. Scott? If it was Scott, then we may surmise that poetics preceded politics for you. Look at your vehement response to the insistence on ethnic nationalism in Quebec during the early 1960s, when you said a person should find meaning "within himself, in the world about him, and in the stars above, the dignity, pride, and other well-springs of poetry . . ."

Then there was the Charter of Rights and Freedoms, our Constitution. And there were your four children, and your devotion to them.

Finally there came your trenchant critiques in your so-called retirement (the time when I knew you) of the powers that be. These were the organizations or beliefs or social and political structures that prevent people from dreaming of the future, and that limit their capacity to be free and intelligent. Let us remember that intelligence for you didn't mean logic. It was another word for mind and heart together, or again for the higher self.

Let us ponder, what is mind? . . . consciousness observing, reflecting on its own existential evolutions . . . And heart? . . . inklings of the ineffable, the intangible soul-trace . . .

"What are we doing here, and why are our hearts invisible?" Anne Carson wrote. Perhaps consciousness is the arrow, heart is the unseen bow. One is sharpened to arrive at a point; the other must be played, and tugged. Mind is always in action, ideas and impressions spinning in the discharge we call thinking. The heart is the crux of the cosmos, the soul opening to the pulse that moves our blood, and the stars.

"In what way is the ineluctable play of the energies of the heart less physically real than the principle of universal attraction?" Teilhard de Chardin asked in *The Phenomenon of Man*. The heart has its energy and fields. Make heart and mind one, and we may approach what you, Pierre, meant by "reason."

Sometimes your heart cooled and your warrior ferocity erupted when you engaged a matching rage. Images haunt me: I see your stillness when you stood your ground against the riot on June 24, 1968, in Montreal, during the St. Jean Baptiste Day celebrations. The RIN (*Rassemblement pour l'indépendance nationale*) bombarded

Mystic Trudeau / 7

the stands with bottles and trash. "Trudeau to the gallows!" they screamed. You were asked to leave by security officials. You refused. In this we saw your steel. The results of your militant anger could be devastating: the implementation of the War Measures Act in 1970, the attempts at a planned economy, the isolation of Quebec after the Constitution was patriated in 1982, your dismissive arrogance with those you suspected didn't share your understanding of the movements of mind. When your heart warmed, and mind was at its service, then we received the Charter and our polyethnic mix, the sublime and courageous policy of many languages and open borders.

But Pierre, what was the moment when you began to deepen? Was it your time at Harvard, then in Europe? Did the intensification of your soul occur during your journey to the East, and you spent Christmas at the mouth of the Ganges? "I read the masses, sang the hymns and generally spent the day in deep meditation," you said in 1948. What revelation came upon you?

This thawing happened after an ugly intellectual start. A spoiled young man in an elite school in Quebec, you spewed ideas rank with fascist anti-Semitism. Yet one day—another inspired moment unknown to us—you chose to wear a red rose in your lapel, the symbol of flowering intensities. Surely the fire came in the rage that says nothing is settled. The world will break open from the force of a transforming dream. Energy comes through the opened eye, intensifying the need to see beyond cliché, our conditioned frames of understanding.

Perhaps you knew that the rose stands for the mystery of identity. The mystic rose represents spiritual expansion, and the quest to find out who we can be. Flowers don't resemble their seeds. Torn from its roots, the rose becomes a symbol that says beginnings and endings radically differ.

You came to fiercely believe that the Universal Spirit would provide guiding brilliance. It's this light that informs us there must be more to our actions than we often recognize. There is the mystery of our selves, and the greater Mystery: what we must do with our selves.

Pierre, you chose to move into politics, thus onto history's plane. But the red rose on your lapel pointed to the mythic dimension, a public passion.

Myth is the realm of the ungovernable translated into symbols and tales. A moment becomes mythic when we sense the ineffable erupting in it. Through the images that form from that crossroads, the inexhaustible speaks.

History is the recitation of events and actions. But mythic knowledge comes when we confront the Sphinx. This is the crucial time when we find ourselves at a crossroads, and we must choose a path. At the juncture, riddling questions come to the pilgrim—always in three parts, striking out of light and darkness: Who are you? From where have you come? Where are you going? We call this the arrival of vertical information, or soul knowledge. The vertical abruptly presses down into the horizontal plane, which is history, the domain of matter.

In lives of mythic depth the soul vividly blazes. We shiver with fear and wonder when the soul appears at risk. It is those moments when the vertical and horizontal together form a crux, in the shape of a T, a Y, an X, or a cross. In these cardinal points we see and hear the overtones of the word "crisis."

We have been informed in your biographies that you planned to enter history. "I must become a great man," you wrote in 1940, with a young man's fervour. Biographers express surprise. They say you deceived people. "There is a certain charm to surrounding oneself with mystery," you wrote in a 1939 diary entry. You became evasive, masking yourself—sometimes in a cape and an outlandish hat— but always preparing for the moment when you could act. In your inwardness we find a radical, even an exalted, sense of path. You guarded this, nurturing it, waiting. There would be distractions, doubts.

Yet the moment was waiting for you too.

You spent years thinking, questioning, absorbing, reading, travelling, distancing yourself from your past. "To study pleases me, therefore I study," you declared in 1945. Relentlessly pushing yourself, you honed your polemical skills, and cultivated your personality. One of your lovers, Thérèse Gouin, in bewilderment, called you "*cette étrange construction*," this strange construction. Follow the inkling, the call, the trace, the wave, into the open, and one will surely be impelled to make "an unprecedented conceptual structure" (Nietzsche).

Suddenly, after the long education, when the times appeared right, your image in the electronic media burned into our consciousness. I know from what you told me how this image imprint often astonished you. Yet you became the Canadian TV statesman, the first to understand (or merely use?) the searing webs of association that stream from our screens.

Electricity is the other fire, welding new configurations through the media, lightening paths with overwhelming expansions of implication, meaning breathing everywhere. In that fire we may awaken to illuminations, and to devastations—the revelation of global intimacy.

Electricity and identity: these are the meridians where we find ourselves. Into our lives pour visions, like hallucinations, from screens, from images. Into our lives pour voices from speakers. Our living rooms and workstations are intersections of mutuality, reception centres of grace and vibration. Think of how we name our rooms "living" spaces, the imperative present in the verb acting like an adjective.

We see images turn quickly into symbols, and symbols turn into haunting presences. We hear voices turning into constant companions, sounds and words always whispering in our ears. In the electronic cosmos every moment potentially becomes a crucial here and now. These intersections we could call a crisis; we could say they are a summoning. We are one part in our bodies, one part in the air. Through the streams of energy, beamed directly into our rooms, comes the soul's eternal question, the breath that forms the word "who?"

> There is no need for you to leave the house. Stay at your table and listen. Don't even listen, just wait. Don't even wait, be completely quiet and alone. The world will offer itself to you to be unmasked; it can't do otherwise; in raptures it will writhe before you.

Mystic Trudeau / 11

So Franz Kafka, reluctant seer, envisioned our condition long before anyone, when he wrote that 1918 passage in The Blue Octavo Notebooks.

Pierre, your unfolding endures because those who witnessed your fire think they knew you. Agree or disagree with your vision, each may tell a story of how your ideas, and images of you, entered into their lives. Something indelibly singed us. The e-cosmos spills over with data, merging us with world-feeling. It makes vivid actors like you lastingly familiar, although most may never have actually met you.

Yet for others you are passing into ghostlier demarcations, beginning to fade.

I have long dreamed of a book that would reveal the hidden elements of personality. It would be a book moving away from chronology and history towards mystical biography, the contours and mythologies of spirit and soul.

I've often thought of a book that would catch the vitalist waves of the e-cosmos. It would dispense with linear sequence, and work with epiphanies and radiances, incidents and traces of dialogue, in expanding spheres of learning and knowing.

Could you set a book free to do both?

That's why, Pierre, there must be for me one more visitation. It is to contemplate and engage your enigma and apparition, your spirit and symbol, these considerable complexities. And to answer for myself, and to remember (in the way my dreaming back will permit), why a private man let the fire of intelligence overrule his limitations and occasional hesitations, and placed the red rose—also a symbol of awakening and of vigilance—on his jacket lapel; then launched himself often ruthlessly into the meetings and clashes that incursions into experience must bring.

You became an incognito mystic. And you lived a metaphysical story before people who didn't always grasp your point of reference. In your imagination you considered yourself singled out, even marked.

In this process, strange and powerful, you were a person who lived in history, in fact; and you became a persona who entered our imaginations with the energy of fiction, and thus became a part of our dream of ourselves, in our time and place. The meridians of identity and electricity, and of poetry and experience, continue to seize me.

Old friend, you broke into public and into Canadian myth. By doing so you addressed our spiritual fire. And you spoke of vision, the time when we too would let our minds and hearts open.

First Call

When I first wanted to talk to Trudeau in 1984, he had become notoriously evasive. A silence had descended over him in his retirement. "Silence is my way out and I always take refuge in it," he wrote in 1941, in his journal. Privacy would always be his shield. Evasiveness was his way of insulating his highly sensitive personality (so I'd learn) against demands for explanation.

Nevertheless, I was working on a book in which he prominently figured, and I needed to cap the essay on him with a meeting.

There seemed to be no way to get to him.

I tried contacts through the Liberal Party. These had come in part because my father had been in the 1950s an executive assistant to the Minister of Mines and Resources under Prime Minister St. Laurent. In the early 1960s my father was a part of Cell 13, a group of reform-minded activists established by Lester Pearson to help implement the goals of Walter Gordon. Oddly, considering that they had travelled in similar political circles, my father had never met Trudeau.

The contacts, senators and members of Parliament, were helpful in voicing support, and little else. Finally, it was Senator Keith Davey who offered to speak directly to Trudeau, with the recommendation that we meet. Davey was, he told me later on the phone, rebuked by Trudeau.

"Why should I make an exception for this young man?" This was how Davey reported Trudeau's sharp response.

On the advice of my friend, Teri (T.C.) McLuhan—daughter of Marshall McLuhan, an author herself—I decided to write to him. She'd said,

"Pierre likes the direct route. Here's his home address. Write a letter to him. Tell him who you are and what you want to do. He'll either answer, or he won't. . . . I'll speak to him too. . . . What do you have to lose?"

My letter (the draft long misplaced now) was lengthy, and cheeky. I told him about the book I was planning, the ideas I hoped to present, the style and form I wanted to achieve, how he should make an exception for me.

I typed a shorter version.

This one was more to the point. Perhaps he'd respond to the tone and the pitch.

I hesitated, read it over, tightened it again, and then sealed it in an envelope.

At the mailbox near the corner of the downtown street where I lived at that time in Toronto, I hesitated again. Before I dropped the letter in, I thought,

"This is a lost cause."

I doubted if he'd reply.

Better a lost cause than no cause at all, I thought, so I sent the letter off. And I went back to my home, and to writing other stories.

*

1985.

Two weeks after I sent the letter, I received a phone call at my desk.

"Mr. Powe?"

I said yes.

"Gisele Brooke, personal assistant to Pierre Trudeau."
The voice on the line was accented, briskly formal.
I was silent.
"Mr. Powe?"
My silence must have been long.
"Yes?"
"You're still there. Good. Mr. Trudeau is on the line. Would you care to speak to him?"

Maybe this was a joke. I had several friends who were expert mimics. Trudeau was easy to parody. (Only Elvis was easier.)

Static on the line crackled, becoming louder.

I realized that I'd said little. Finally I said, too quickly, "Certainly, yes, please."

An awing pause.

On came the voice.

"Bruce."

He spoke as if he already knew me.

"I've read your letter closely. And I liked how it sounded. Your ideas interest me. I went to the library and took out your first book. I read it, and quite liked it." (I was on guard with that modifying "quite.") "Your idea about your new book isn't what I usually see. It's much more . . . literary. So I thought we should talk, at least here. If you wish. And if you're not too busy."

Those last sentences had an acerbic tinge, unmistakably his mark. I was convinced. It was Trudeau.

"Teri McLuhan spoke of you. We have Marshall McLuhan in common, I believe?"

I told him how I'd been one of McLuhan's students in the last class he gave at the University of Toronto.

"A great mind," he said.

A pause while he seemed to gather his thoughts.

"I don't do interviews."

That flattening statement was reminiscent of dismissive shrugs he gave at press conferences. Was the promising start to our conversation over?

"But . . ."

He waited (for effect?).

". . . if you would like to have lunch together, that would be fine. We can talk over a meal. A conversation is much better than an interview, don't you think?"

I readily agreed, and thought, now what? He went on,

"Would you like me to come to Toronto to see you, or would you like to come to Montreal and meet me here?"

There was (surprising to me then) a curious graciousness to his tone. He sounded as if he was trying to be courteous, even to please.

"I'd be happy to come to Montreal."

"Good. We can have a nice long lunch and a long talk. Speak to my assistant, Gisele Brooke. She'll make the arrangements."

I thought the conversation was over, but there was more.

"You know," he began, almost shyly. "I've been out of touch with literature for many years. All I had to read, most of the time, were government documents. Briefs, reports, that sort of thing. And I'm sure you know how dull that material can be."

"Without style."

"Without anything like intellectual challenge or style. But that's what took up my attention. Many of my colleagues didn't read much either." He was sharp again. "Now I have time to read. . . . Who is Elias Canetti? That's one writer you mentioned in your letter. I haven't heard of him."

I said how much I admired Canetti's pivotal work, *Crowds and Power*, and then we talked of writers and writing.

"So many books to read," he said.

He used verbal shorthand, often caustic, sometimes mild, a quick style with which I would become familiar.

"Could you make up a list for me? What do you think I should be reading? Poetry, essays, philosophy, novels, whatever you think. Of course, I have much more time now. You know, I came to miss the time I once had to read, and to be alone."

I said it would be my pleasure to come up with a list, and I promised that I would bring it when we met in Montreal.

"Good, I'll see you here soon."

"With the list of books."

"It'll give us more to talk about," he said.

He passed me on to his assistant, and I set up the times when we were to meet.

This was the beginning of our long conversation. The meetings would form for me a pattern of crucial intersections, offering moments where meaning would emerge.

Over the years of our contact I kept a sometimes fragmentary record of what was said, and what was done.

All these reflections, and addresses, are reconstructed from my notes. They have been changed by the perspectives that have changed in me, and in our times.

Yet they have become my way of finding him again.

He is still there, in these words, speaking up from what I've written down.

Crossroads

1989.

"Shall we look at our fortunes?" Trudeau asked.

We were at the Chinese restaurant around the corner from his office, in Montreal.

"Let's see what our destinies might bring," he said.

Taunting smile. Some Brahman knowledge. His stare that appeared to ask, What will you dare?

We cracked open the cookies. His slip read, *You would make a good lawyer.*

Looking aggrieved, Trudeau snapped back in his chair as if he was turning away from an offence, his right hand placed protectively on his heart.

"I already am a good lawyer." He was emphatic. "I don't need to be told that . . ." He paused. His aggrieved look continued. Then he leaned forward. ". . . But what does yours say? Let me see." He was stern. Perhaps mine would be equally irrelevant, or surprising.

I showed him the slip. It was blank.

"How did you manage that?" he asked. "Do you know someone here?"

"You think I have extra influence? Here. I'll trade with you," I said.

He laughed.

"Well, it's a good fortune for a writer. The blank page waiting for a beginning." His look turned mischievous. "Keep them both. For your records."

And so I did, until both strips disintegrated into dust.

*

1998.

Another lunch, at the Chrysanthemum, a Chinese restaurant again, near his office.

"Let's examine our destinies, once more . . ." Trudeau was quiet for a moment. ". . . With all that we have to do." He spoke carefully, his voice edged with irony. He glared, his eyes unblinking.

I had asked him to attend the Trudeau Era Conference, which I was directing along with colleagues at York University in Toronto. He had refused my invitation to come. I had pressed him on this during our lunch, and he had refused again. "It's just not something I want to do at this time," he had said firmly, but with a certain unexpected wistfulness in his tone.

"Here. You open them both."

He smiled and slowly handed me the small plate that held the fortune cookies. I saw his hand tremble. A look of concentration came into his eyes when he passed the plate along. He seemed to be watching attentively to ensure that he wouldn't drop it.

That day, in the autumn of that year, I found him frail. There had been long silences in our conversation.

"Now tell me, what does it say?" he asked.

I opened his slip for him. It said, *You will be travelling soon.* This was true. He had tickets for elsewhere, so he'd told me earlier. Mine read, *You will find a way to overcome obstacles.*

"Interesting," he said.

I waited.

"Once more, yours is better." He was thoughtful. There was another silence. At last he said, "Keep them.

You might find a use for them someday, somewhere."

And I did keep them, until these two slips of paper were also dust.

*

These seemingly light incidents.

They remain with me because through them I'm reminded of the weight that Pierre Trudeau put on the word "destiny."

Destiny implies a calling. The word "calling," with its overtones of hearing and recalling, provokes the questions: What will you follow? What do you pursue? By what energies have you been pressed? What is calling, what is being heard? It also suggests, What do you fear most of all? What will make you turn away from destiny? Follow your heart, the adage says; but then how can any of us know the evolutions and evocations of the heart in the noisy turbulence of day-to-day scrambles.

Consider "calling." It's what we often mean by vocation, and by the gift of genius. "Genius": from the Latin root, *genius*, meaning an inborn nature, a talent, a vital inclination, the guiding charge of a person, our inward guardian. It can mean a spirit talking through you, a transferral of energy. "In-spirit-us"; a calling is therefore an inspiration.

A calling is sometimes understood to be the urging of the daimon, the voice of the Universal Spirit. "Daimon" is an old word that points to the higher intelligence, the Other, that may inform our conduct and pathways. Pascal, one of Trudeau's touchstone philosophers, said the heart has its reasons, which the propositions of the mind can never fully prove. This directs us toward a transcendent first principle (or, again, *noûs*), a source greater than our customary egos. And by ego I mean that which occupies itself with itself, and (necessarily, inevitably) with schedules, cooking, cleaning, working, driving, doing the laundry, attending to partners, children, ailing parents, or neighbours.

Calling means to be lifted, to be transported. You are going somewhere. This inspiration can be theatrical, big. It can seem like dynamite to yourself, and an excruciating nuisance to family members, or lovers. It means making demands on yourself, and on others.

The call is what constitutes the sublime. "I do feel that genius is a power of the soul," Northrop Frye wrote, with his usual poignant and eloquent hope, in his *Notebooks and Lectures on the Bible and Other Religious Texts*, "and that the powers of the soul can be developed by everyone . . ."

Calling and destiny appear the same. It is whatever breathes into you suddenly. It is what hints, speaks, murmurs, informs or spells, bellows or shouts, hauntingly in the night, or quickly in the morning, and takes you by surprise, demanding that you acknowledge for yourself, "I must be, I must be." (In the mantra words of Saul Bellow's Gene Henderson, "*I want, I want.*") To call is to summon. Thus we rise or bring forth, we are brought or led forward. The mind ripples like stirring waves. You hear, you receive; you recall, you evoke. The moment is like an intersecting crossroad; and the moment is metaphysical—something outside of the physical flows in, or down, into us.

Destiny has archaic reverberations. It is probably dismissed by most; we may think of it primarily in terms of heroes and warriors, shamans and soothsayers, apostles and martyrs, artists and inventors. But the reverberation for some can be groundbreaking. It can mean the creation of an individual myth, a metaphor or story to live by. A transfigured self comes through, on the waters of the chaos we know to be life.

A vocation may become a violation. The inner mandate insists on a lack of mediation. You talk directly to the powers, you receive immediately. A calling may tell you, transcend what you deem to be the restrictions of, say, an audience, a public, a city-state, a career, a family.

Let us echo Rainer Maria Rilke: one day you stand up, and start walking. You may get up uneasily, or you may leap up with enthusiasm; you may be shaky, you may be confident. You keep going, walking towards a mountain, a spring, a desert, a river, a forest, a shrine, a castle, a theatre, a studio, a palace of justice, the place of governance. You could wake up and start moving towards someone you felt the necessity to meet. That genius, or daimon, tells you to follow an internal narrative—an idealized route, no doubt—perhaps incommunicable, even absurd, to other people observing. We can say the moment of the calling is a mystical seed. Mysticism, we also say, is the desire to know what is within, and what is beyond us.

An epiphany comes, saying "You must change." It could feel like "thunder on the mountain," Bob Dylan sang. You feel uncovered. (And you may even feel like you are sitting exposed in an open field with the sun like a spotlight on your skin.) It may have all happened rapidly, too rapidly. Then you might lose track. What was it? It's as if you've heard a window or a door open somewhere. Are you inside, or outside? It's very much the modern script to believe yourself to be confused, or merely deluded, by the uncovering. So, move on, ignore the signs. Some people don't ignore the signs or the stirrings. They pick them up eagerly. The signs are indicators of direction. Follow these. It's time for the whole person to be moved.

*

At a point, once again obscure to us, Trudeau woke up, and began approaching a sign ahead of him. He became something other than the narrow Catholic Quebec nationalist that he was when he was an insular youth attending the private Jesuit school, Collège Jean-de-Brébeuf. He read deeply in literature, Paul Claudel, Mallarmé, Stendhal, Tolstoy, Baudelaire, Victor Hugo, Arthur Rimbaud. He would later say that he had initially read more deeply in poetry than he had in the economic theories of John Maynard Keynes. He would be moved by God-haunted visionaries, the addled experimenters and iconoclasts. He was transfixed by the nineteenth-century apocalyptics who were themselves incessant questioners, knocking on the door of the ultimate. A persistent questioning of everything is a form of mental savagery. The visionaries he read were gripped by the inklings of an imminent time when humanity would be compelled to confront its destiny. Thus Trudeau read, and read, notated, and read. Reading itself became part of the quest.

He would discover Emmanuel Mounier's philosophy of Personalism. At the centre of all things must stand the human soul, he came to believe. The soul, though, is like a seed. It's given, but not yet enriched or fulfilled. It has to feed on light. It has to have a compass, and it has to be strengthened. The body itself must be trained. All this because the soul is like a fire inside a stone; it has to be struck, and then released. He would educate himself, and go to Harvard (1944 to 1946), to l'École libre des sciences politiques in Paris (1946 to 1947), to the London School of Economics (1947 to 1948), and then set out on his travels, through Eastern Europe, the Middle East, India and the East (1948 to 1949). In Paris, he would encounter the ideas of the mystic philosophers Henri Bergson and Pierre Teilhard de Chardin. It would be from Teilhard that he would learn of the evolutionary "noosphere," how the world is a pulse, glowing towards cosmic realization. In London he studied under Harold Laski (who would inspire the poet Irving Layton). With Laski he would explore the intersections of Christianity and Socialism. He heard of the world becoming "a free city." And he would make notes, and he would think, and he would continue to absorb influences, and he would travel, intellectually, spiritually, imaginatively, physically. He would walk through deserts and jungles.

He was constantly crossing borders.

In the mid-1950s and into the early 1960s, there was a period of seeming drift. But drift can be a fallowing time. He wrote, walked in strike-lines, taught, helped to found *Cité libre*, lectured, argued, travelled, went canoeing, practised law, dated many women. He was by all reports unsettled—in teaching, in law, in Quebec, in love.

Trudeau turned to politics, not to academia or literature. Politics became for him his calling. It was his form of world loyalty, a spirit compulsion. Cosmopolitanism would be his inspiration and his metaphysical lure, the energy that broadened him, pulling him away from his provincial upbringing. The primary revolution—the first and deepest revolt—must occur in the mind and the heart.

Trudeau wrote this, in 1940, while he was a student at Harvard,

> Intelligence: to think for one self; admit the truth. Peace means living in harmony, recognizing the rights and responsibilities of others. To do that, one must do one's own thinking freed from the yoke of public opinion.

Intelligence: this word emerges from the Latin *intellectus*, suggesting perception, understanding. It means to make choices—stand in the crux, and step forward. Curiously, "intelligence" is related to "legend," and to "wisdom." "Intelligibility" alludes to the capacity to follow a route; or, I presume, the willingness (a.k.a. the courage) to obey the intimations of the higher self. It implies a breaking through.

Perception: it means to pierce. Things dawn on you, like morning light, and the sun's rising. You open your eyes. This is the first circle. Then you close your eyes, in the evening of awareness. In that moment you may still see spheres of light, white specks on a black background. Then light fades, and you approach the dark. Open your eyes, and the cycle, like the day and the night, begins again. James Joyce caught this pattern in his daylight vision, *Ulysses*, and in his nightlight vision, *Finnegans Wake*. They are complementary pieces that evoke the power of the imagination guiding its way towards recognitions of codes at work. Each time you truly open your eyes and your mind, the pattern deepens.

Trudeau trusted that if you shifted borderlines, read, studied, made mental excursions, set out into a wilderness, paddled along a river, a pattern—a code—would reveal itself. What was the code? Pilgrimage . . . Once you voyaged, however, you wouldn't come back in the same way. There will be signs but few useful maps. Others made the maps, and you have to make your own. All the signs will be, must be, metaphors, not theories.

No rebellious heart is ever at ease with paths established by others. Such a soul will be perpetually at odds, often with itself. The calling to personal pilgrimage may bring elevated clarity, but it will also bring conflicted relationships with traditional orders, and their directives.

Here is Trudeau, writing in 1941, preparing himself, and showing off for whoever may have been listening, or (so he hoped) was reading over his shoulder,

> . . . pride presumes another that is much more presumptuous, because it presumes that people will take the trouble to read what we write on scraps of paper, that some day biographers will delve into all that we have written down to follow therein the development of our thinking. One knows instinctively just how foolish that assumption is. And so, rebelling against oneself, one picks up the pen and writes. But even

that rebellion is rooted in pride: it is inspired not so much from believing impossible our future greatness and the need for biographers, but rather from thinking it very unlikely that these biographers (who, we hope, will have to exist), will even take the huge trouble to study the immense accumulation of paper that we are gathering . . .

Pride, we surmise, would be for Trudeau a synonym for the compulsion to prepare ("Readiness is all"). It was also another word for aspiration. It would be his virtue, and his vice; he would press himself, and press others. Every time is crucial if one chooses to make it so. In 1944 he wrote, "To relearn how to think." We may smile skeptically at his young dreams of intellectual heroism (and wonder if in his hours spent huddled over books, plotting scenarios of greatness, he had read too much Thomas Carlyle). Yet we also see in his actions and in his notes the hunger for breadth, and for breath, the broadening of being. We feel momentum in his soul's urgings. And we sense the looming contests. His mysticism will help to make him charismatic. It will lead him into fiery engagements, raging disputes. He was writing scripts for the self.

I kept the scraps of paper from lunches that took place many years ago, thinking they would be mere mementoes. They would surely be reminders of the times I spent talking to a man, by then a former Prime Minister, who I'd grown up admiring for his decisive reshaping of my country.

The scraps of paper became more. They came to be symbolic references to intersections with one who had asked us to write our own scripts, and who had himself traced his way towards a complex and conflicted eminence.

Calling

From an early age I felt from afar the importance of Trudeau's political engagement. The sense of calling in him was impossible to ignore. It was about more than politics. It was about mind, intelligence, society and culture directed towards a new kind of inspired consciousness. These intensities rippled through the TV screen in shadowy black-and-white images that emanated into the 1960s.

Through images we observed him, and through soundtracks we absorbed him. In images (moving and still) he became known to us. The e-cosmos is ensouled—animated, omnipresent; and information was overflowing even then, on small TVs with their wraithlike pictures, and on small radios with their staticky mono speakers. Spots of time erupted in vulnerable households.

"The media involves mythically, in depth, instantaneously, at the speed of light," Marshall McLuhan said. Trudeau appeared from the beginning in the beams of the media now, provoking us with ideas and ironies. He flippantly gestured, and smiled as if he knew something more than he said. This intimated changes to come. The cosmos seemed to me—and continues to seem to me—to be raining and sometimes ramming its way through screens, in an unprecedented pulse of presences and pressures. This is how all of us share an original relation with vibration itself. He was part of the streaming and the mood of electric connection.

Let us say that when we engage images and symbols, the seeming, the appearance, is all. And because I am peculiarly impressionable, and (sometimes inexplicably to myself) susceptible to the sway of moods and images, I was struck by Trudeau's difference from other Canadians and political leaders. I wanted to be a writer, and yet the shadows on the screens held me in their thrall. I had glimpses of how life could be strangely suffused by overshadowing apparitions. It seemed to me that we, in our historical period, had come to an apex. Our souls were rising. We experienced affinities directly in the waves of information. The borders that mattered would be the ones we drew between ourselves and the energy fields we call electricity. (Though how could we set a limit to the flow, so much like the flow of mind?) We needed, so I thought, to school ourselves in what the images and soundtracks said.

"The medium is the message." The screens and speakers were charismatic mediation points, through which universal emotion and symbols unrolled. They embodied, and channelled, the implications of world-feeling. Waves of energy were plurality itself.

Trudeau was inside this whirlwind drive. His actions and the images we received of him seemed to insist that government had to be part of the process when the soul's rise was apparent again. What was this emergence? It was "the vertical passion" (James Hillman), wisdom, imagination, intelligence, perception, carrying inklings of the spiritual trace. Ignoring this call left us adrift—and worse, in peril. Apogees and gulfs would haunt us. We would stare into paradise, and pandemonium.

Trudeau embodied a portion of the time's pressure and calling. Whether this was a historical accident (he happened to look and act right), or whether this was projection and opportunism (we needed a figure like him, he cunningly obliged) wasn't important to me then. Life had a hold of him, and he was willing to follow it. Images were speaking to us, and we were following them.

In the rawness of those moments, Trudeau said the destiny of a country was to be a just society.

The phrase was blurted, I now think. It must have surged up spontaneously, surprising a person who tended to premeditate most of his utterances. It came up from the deepest sources of his learning and pilgrimages. It is reverberating in us even still.

*

1989.

We stood on the street outside the office building which housed Heenan Blaikie. This was the law firm that he worked for after his retirement from the Liberal leadership in 1984.

"When will you come back to Montreal again?" he asked.

I was thanking him for our time over lunch, saying goodbye.

"Bring more books, and we'll talk again about biographies and poetry," he said.

People crowded by, recognizing him.

A burly man, mysteriously wearing a huge fur coat (it was summer), grabbed him and announced,

"Why man, you're the coolest."

I glanced around for a security presence. Perhaps there were RCMP plainclothes officers nearby? I saw none. (And I never saw any security over the years. He preferred to make himself available on the streets. I have since wondered whether he simply wasn't concerned about his safety. This was another dare to whatever, or whoever, was out there.)

Trudeau smiled, genuinely taken aback, and then returned the hearty embrace. He was much smaller than the man in the coat, so he looked like he was about to disappear into the fur.

A fashionably dressed woman deliberately bumped into him.

"Oh, excuse me," she said. She then lingered long enough to get his autograph.

"It's hard to talk out here." He stated the obvious, once the burly man and the woman had gone.

I said I would be back soon, though I never knew when I would return to Montreal. These were the years when I was struggling to establish myself in writing, in teaching, and I had little money for excursions anywhere.

When I paused, perhaps suggesting to him that I wasn't sure if I was welcome, he said,

"I always set aside time for our conversations."

*

So I've set aside time to contemplate what you meant to me, and to us.

Pierre, the conversation continues.

At Harvard, in your room at Perkins Hall, you wrote "Pierre Trudeau, Citizen of the World" over your door.

It was one of your signal announcements.

"Like Emerson, I write over the door of my library the word 'Whim,'" Oscar Wilde wrote. This was, for Wilde, the sign of dissenting inwardness. It revealed how much he planned to trust his daimon, following the inner voice wherever it might lead.

The Stoic philosopher Diogenes coined the phrase "citizen of the world." "Citizen" reverberated with the bold credos of individual rights.

Pierre, the sign you placed over your door, in your student dorm, was more than a prank. It was an idea. (Wilde again: "Yes, it is dangerous—all ideas, as I told you, are so.") Did it represent the beginning of your move towards the cosmopolitanism you would espouse for Canadians? Here are the implications: walk away from roots, from one culture, from anything monolithic, or monotone. Come forward into the many—thoughts are infinite—and journey on. This rootlessness would be especially vital in the image and symbol world-sphere that the media was creating.

To be uprooted means to be elsewhere. Thus it means to cultivate a difference, to seek, willingly at times, a distancing from others. It also suggests the imperative of re-creating yourself: making yourself new (you are the poem, while the poem lasts). All this evokes the supremacy of the personal, the apogee that is the individual soul. That is not the same as saying that the individualist him- or herself is supreme. Individualism could lead to greed and self-indulgence. However, the idea of the personal is subtle: it means the directives of the higher self must be understood beyond social, linguistic, ethnic, cultural roots or borderlines. Kabbalah names this calling the *neshamah*, the transcendent self in its exalted, cognitive aspect.

But Pierre, when you became active in politics, and eventually Prime Minister, you were attacked for your espousal of rootless cosmopolitanism.

You were condemned for your supposed foreignness. By renouncing the purely provincial, you embraced the new wilderness; and it is electronic, multilingual, interracial, the planet-pulsing. It must have looked to others like an embrace of chaos. Anything beyond the borderlines of a settlement is a jungle, a desert, a sea, a galaxy.

Critics called you the stranger. You were said to be not really "one of us" in English Canada. Some said you became the leader who never understood his own country. Critics liked to moralize with you, and to chidingly psychoanalyze you. There must be something wrong with someone who so wilfully refused to fit in. They attacked you for your skepticism over anything to do with "nations." You were boxed in by those who liked to categorize. They branded you a contrarian, someone uneasily ambivalent about his background, too willing to make demands of people who didn't want to be irritated, or bothered. You were too assertively private in the midst of growing and aggressive collectivities. Some said your Charter of Rights and Freedoms, and your faith in a multilingual, multi-ethnic society, would destroy the foundations of the country. This was a point where Quebec separatists and ethnocentric English Canadians found agreement.

Your vision of the cultural, political process was complex, and cunning. Here, one could retain a portion of the old—whatever world one may have come from—and yet become the new—the being who breaks from the past.

The lack of borderlines was a sign of openness. In the lexical clusters that expand from the original word "open" we find these words and phrases—"unclosed," "clear," "clearing," "free access," "the lifting of the curtain," "a door latch lifting," "unbounded," "facing upwards." We find "undone," and "wound." "Open," etymologies say, is a relative of "up."

It was these qualities and advocacies that hooked me. The power to re-create one's self, outside of family or background, or institution or language, is the enduring legacy of radical being and imagination. William Blake and Percy Shelley, avatars of the Romantic spirit, called reason "the calculating faculty," and placed imagination above it. Yet we may say that their faith in the daimon of inspiration, in the genius of internal narrative, could be understood to be a variation—or a deflecting rearticulation—of the light of principle. Poetic metaphor and fable can become a technique for initiating the task or quest, following identity's trail, in its suggestive arrangements and provocative dimensions.

Pierre, I submit that all this is part of your legacy. Allow mind, *noûs* or light, to move us, and we will surely find ourselves carried elsewhere.

*

1989.

Over lunch at the Chinese restaurant (again), we talked about philosophy.

"Reason over passion." I wanted to know more about what he meant when he advocated this. It was a phrase mocked in the press, by political foes and by allies alike and by people who had once been close to him.

"Plato said the two great universal forces are reason and necessity." He spoke with the kind of exacting critical distinctions that he liked to apply in this sort of discussion.

"Reason is . . . what? . . . Rationality?" I replied.

"No." He looked ready to pounce. "Reason is mind." He paused. "It's guidance and light. We could call it lucidity."

He sat thinking.

Then he said, "It's what I understand to be intelligence." A special stress on the word "intelligence." His stare across the table was level, evaluating.

I pondered, waiting to see if he would extend his thoughts.

Then I said, "And the mind will see through. Mind will perceive, over and above the passions that dislocate us. Passion in this sense being . . . what? Out-of-control emotions?"

There was no hesitation in his reply.

"Mind meaning that reason will prevail, but how it does so may be a mystery to us. An enigma. I think of reason as being the call to justice."

We stopped there, and went on with our meal.

It was a lot to process.

I wasn't ready at that time to truly comprehend some of what he said. However, I did know that reason and necessity would inevitably battle one another. Sensational, traumatic crossroads of experience (in politics, in the media, in allegiances, in marriages and their failures or disappointments) could upset and bury, if not belittle or betray, any sense of light, or reason, or imaginative recreation, or mindfulness, or justice.

I propose that what Trudeau meant was this: the light of principle always appears to others (and perhaps to oneself) in ways that seem enigmatic. Callings are never wholly comprehended, even by the one who feels called. The Platonic ideal he spoke of was grounded in his spiritual faith—the Thomist was speaking that day through him, over lunch—that the light of mind and heart is benign. (And that this light wasn't a form of repressed memory, in Freudian terms.) This faith informed him. "And all shall be well and/All manner of thing shall be well," T.S. Eliot wrote in "Little Gidding." Eliot was resetting a prayer by Julian of Norwich, in the sequence he called *Four Quartets*. Trudeau had committed these lines to memory. They confirmed his hope that the light in the mind burned to direct us towards the good.

Reason was greater than logic. It was higher consciousness. It was the spiritual cord, or the metaphysical connective. This compelled existential heroism. "See, judge, act," Mounier taught. Reason was the guardian conscience, the mentoring spirit. The Universal Spirit must be harmonized with the physical body (the embodiment of the horizontal plane), so that movement towards the good would become possible. If the Universal Spirit joins with the mortal lower self, then being becomes rational: all in ratio—whole. One breathes, and acts.

Trudeau's faith in the light of reason was tempered by his readings of Isaiah Berlin. In these readings, Trudeau would find Berlin's advocacy for plurality, modest liberty, for decency, and a cautious welcome to the new. Platonic idealism could turn to Absolutism, and monstrousness. Overweening pride in one's sense of calling can lead to stubborn arrogance. Reason would then be blinded to anything but its own inexorable requirements.

Justice must be the agenda that always remains unfinished. Why? The danger for pluralistic societies would be to have one person's notion of justice imposed above all others.

Living brings its savage, often poignant, ironies. Trudeau's marriage to the young Margaret Sinclair dramatically unravelled in public in the 1970s. (Trudeau met her, when she was nineteen, in 1967, in Tahiti. What was their first conversation about? Plato.) Estranged, and enraged, she wrote two volumes of memoirs, *Beyond Reason* and *Consequences*. They are more like apologias than memoirs. The first volume's title contained a blatant challenge to her ex-husband's disciplined devotion to ideas. It also represented a jab at his urgings to think and look beyond. *Consequences* was a later moralistic self-corrective, her *mea magna culpa*. One volume might have been surely titled *Exercising My Rights*; the second volume should have been entitled *Learning Responsibilities*. Trudeau was known to stare at the covers of these books—if he spied someone holding them—with anger he couldn't conceal.

*

How ironic and strange it is to also find how many biographers and historians want to finally resolve the enigma of his soul, and complete our picture of him.

In Monique and Max Nemni's *Young Trudeau: Son of Quebec, Father of Canada, 1919–1944*, the authors, while deeply sympathetic to their subject, were formidably honest in their research. They revealed shocking information about Trudeau's youthful intellectual flirtations. He had suppressed, or omitted, references to this period in his life. But the Nemnis discovered an early strain in him of fascistic bigotry. They described his attachment to religious—read: Catholic—doctrinaire supremacy. He had a period, when he was a student, when he believed in Quebecois collective exceptionalism; his teenage beliefs had been gripped by rightist revolutionary zealotry. The unearthing of his play *Dupés*, written in 1938, exposed a boy who didn't hesitate to link "politics and Jews" in a way that appalls. Here are the Nemnis, in their concluding passage,

> A long established myth presents the image of Pierre Trudeau who, even in his early years, was unable to submit to authority, who always rowed against the current . . . We hope that this first volume of his biography will have laid to rest all such speculation by demonstrating that the enigma has always been nothing but a fiction. . . . The true mystery is how he traveled from a vision of the nation that was organic, ethnic, and communitarian, to the vision of a society that is based on citizenship, that is pluralist and liberal . . . Resolving this second mystery [is] no small undertaking . . .

Trudeau should be held accountable for reprehensible opinions; everyone should be. But his beginning was not his end. And from awful experiences came redemptive action, new representations of identity. If there is nothing conclusive in the unbinding of the self, then there is the liberty to become. What is the free mind but intellectual growth? Thought itself is motion.

And can one resolve a mystery? Should we wish to do so? What is the power of myth to one urged on by the internal voice? Why are myth and fiction (and therefore poetry) synonymous with falsehood in the passage above?

If you can completely explain something, then it stops being a mystery. And when it stops being a mystery, the process stops being a quest.

The Sphinx

Here is a myth: the Sphinx poses a stalling, murderous riddle to the pilgrim at the dire crossroads. The Sphinx is hybrid, multiple, three-in-one, a tripartite beast, lion, winged creature, human. Its questions come in the three parts, "What crawls in the morning? . . . walks upright at noon? . . . walks on three legs in the evening?" The great beast carries the great code in its questions about identity, because in these questions once more we find the implied "who?," and the implicit "Who are you?"

Disquieted, the pilgrim gives an answer, of a kind. The answer thwarts the beast, but resolves nothing. Another journey must begin. The pilgrim, proclaimed king, marries, and presides over a state. Eventually more troubling questions ensue. The new riddles lead to devastating disclosures. The original reply leads to more riddles, and more mysteries, each intricately enlaced in the other.

After the tragedy, the pilgrim is exiled. He wanders, sightless and cursed. He must tap-tap his way forward, learning to live by insight. (Insight is internal vision, the mind comprehending patterns beyond empirical evidence.) Vision brings searing redemption to the wanderer at a site (Colonus), another crossroad that is neither his starting point nor the state he once led.

"We are Oedipus," Jorge Luis Borges writes in his poem "Oedipus and the Enigma." We tap towards every intersection, where we discover we carry within us both the pilgrim and the beast. The point surely is that there is no end to the arrivals at crossroads, thus no end to questions. Signs never stop visiting us, even if we pay no attention to them. Grant us a soul, and we may begin to grant that it will have its own subterranean track.

The soul, like thought, is in motion. Passions, and emotions, reveal the movements of the spirit.

There is danger in the calling. When summoned, one must step forward. Moshe Idel and Gershom Scholem, comprehensive students of the Kabbalah, have documented warnings about what would happen if one is unprepared at the crossroads, and if one attempts to heed the question, and respond to the riddle, without reflection or guidance. If one rises in the intersection, and tries to trace the dictates of what one perceives to be a spiritual imprint, what may come? Messianic delusion, unenlightened ambition. Spiritual vanity could mislead the pilgrim, leading one down into dementia.

Admonitions abound in the writings that comprise the spiritual corpus. In *The Hermetica*, the Kabbalah, the Gnostic texts, *The Sibyllines*, we find warnings about opening up the mind and senses. Pursue the boundlessness that surpasses understanding, and you could stray too far. "Kabbalah" means "tradition." It implies tissues of white-light connectives, so that being won't be shattered by revelation, or by self-importance. Reckless attempts to bypass accepted routes could lead to transgression, evil energies (rages) which the searcher may unwittingly invite into himself.

At the crossing—a symbol of the meeting of the vertical and the horizontal—you may get down on your knees. This could be a conversion moment (on the road to Damascus). But the deal could be sealed with whatever being you think is there. It could be an exacting contract.

"That's when I went to the crossroads, and made a big deal. Where's this guy been? He's been at the crossroads," so said Bob Dylan. This was his witty explanation of the sudden, seemingly inexplicable flowering of his gift, and the proud self-recognition of his genius, in Martin Scorsese's documentary *No Direction Home*.

When you're at the arduous juncture, the parables tell us, you may meet the Sphinx, the angel, the prophetic guide, the burning bush, the demon. No doubt these are all images, and interpretations, of the same experience of an enigmatic intersection with the Universal Spirit.

In *The Enneads* Plotinus said,

> . . . this vision is hard to describe . . . This is no doubt why in the mysteries we are forbidden to reveal them to the uninitiated . . . [it] cannot be shown to those who have not had the happiness to see it.

Instability could plague the pilgrim. Ostracized, one could slip howling into an abyss. The mind could be ridden by demons into obsession.

Darkness transfigures the soul. A rash heroism will wreak havoc on others, and on oneself. Ego can distort what conscience may be saying. Bestirred, your voice could sound, terribly, like it belongs to someone, or something, else. *Para—nous*, paranoia: it means to be beside yourself, outside the mind's light.

What if you tore reality's veils and saw the soul was hideous?

What if you ripped the veils down, and found the souls of others to be more complex than you could ever have envisioned?

We could be addressed by a void, slivered through with the illusion of things vibrating at perception's edge.

The mind is so powerful it could be gripped by its capacity to generate fictions.

It is for these reasons that Zen masters instruct their

students to be calm and detached. In yogic training openness is shaped by self-mastery and physical dexterity. "Keep watch, and wait . . . Let him beware, too, of the light that weighs," the teachers of enlightenment say. There is more to the cosmos than most can comprehend, or bear. "Innumerable universes tremble at the tip of the Buddha's hair," a Zen maxim says.

*

Pierre, I suspect you learned these truths from your experiences when you travelled, and then in politics, the most unstable of realms. It was better to keep your quest an enigma, because then there could be no resolution, only more engagements, more experience. One would have to delve deeply into the soul, into its images, using one's imagination, the light of reconstruction. "I wanted to know everything and experience everything, in every realm," you wrote in 1993, in your skimpy *Memoirs*. This was a book that gave readers the sense that you weren't concerned with explaining anything in detail. Yet your severe faith in the higher self could lead you to act with startling, disturbing speed. Witness the implementation of the War Measures Act in 1970. And you said to me on different occasions, in restaurants, on the street, "I intend what I said to be enigmatic . . . I was content to play one role, now I'm playing another . . ." (We'd talk these ideas over frequently, in other conversational contexts, in other times.)

History is one thing, the energies of spirit are another.

If one leaves gaps, discontinuities, riddling spaces, breaks in a narrative, if one plays roles and creates fictions (tells stories), one allows the unfinished, the unresolved, to thrive in compelling conundrums. One impels the quest. The pilgrimage becomes the destiny; and the pilgrimage broadens on the roads of unforeseen vistas.

The quest for you, Pierre, was to implement that elusive inspiration that came, suddenly it seems, when you left your native soil, with its pent-up concerns, and you hungered to become a citizen of the world.

*

On the first page of Volume One of their pioneering biography, *Trudeau and Our Times: The Magnificent Obsession*, Christina McCall and Stephen Clarkson wrote,

"He haunts us still."

It was a pithy and original phrase when they first penned it. Since the publication of their book it's been quoted often. Now it's become something of a cliché when people speak of Trudeau.

Clarkson later amended the phrase, after years of consideration, in another context, to read more equivocally,

"He taunts us still."

With this revision Clarkson backed away from the wider implications of that inspired first choice in diction, "haunts." Why Clarkson chose to say "taunts" may be an epic story in itself.

Still, "taunts" indicates an incomplete project, even in Clarkson's alteration. A taunt is a challenge, and a reproach. In the clustering of the word, we find that it includes other meanings, "test," "assail," "agitate," "disquiet" and "mock." Clarkson's revision may be indicating that Trudeau's spirit—and the unfulfilled, perhaps broken process he initiated—continues, like a paternal ghost, to rebuke our hesitations and compromises, mocking our falling back into heartless politics.

In a cliché there is often an archetype lurking, beginning to emerge. McLuhan taught us that a cliché embodies the shape of a larger, enduring form. We could begin to approach the Trudeau persona, and its driven aspirations, more effectively if we rearranged the original phrase that began McCall and Clarkson's book to evoke something larger, and Other. "He was haunted still." Or, stronger yet, "He was haunted by an idea."

Trudeau said that the call for him was to serve. Over time the calling became to justice. This is in part what haunted him, and inspired him.

How did this pilgrimage come to be articulated?

Let us conjecture.

A Just Society

Simone Weil said, in the aphorisms and fragments gathered under the title *Gravity and Grace*,

> It is necessary to uproot oneself . . .
>
> To relate belongs to the solitary spirit. No crowd can conceive relationship . . .
>
> Justice. To be ever ready to admit that another person is something quite different from what we read when he is there (or when we think about him) . . .
>
> Wherever the spirit ceases to be a principle it also ceases to be an end . . .

Weil often struggles in her notebooks to define "justice." It's like trying to define a beautiful mist, or to nail air to a wall. Justice: its sublime tone poses a hypnotic hold on us; though, typically, with such a grand term, it means whatever we will make of it.

Yet I note how suspicious Weil was of that which would coerce the person, obliterating and corrupting our potential for reaching the other side, which she calls supernatural. A Gnostic and a mystic, Weil wrestled with how societies had to be dedicated to allowing the soul the chance to be uprooted from its conditions of material entrapment. An uprooting could lead to cognition. Dormant inside us was the spark of principle. Societies were unjust when they did not permit a person to seek that spark in his or her own sphere. The inspired principle was rebellious gravitation. It was a powerful field bending time and history towards justice. Inspiration, or grace, was necessarily unpredictable, sometimes an ordeal. But one way or another, the call to eminence should fall to everyone. Prohibitions on the potential of grace, in whatever way it appears, were despotic, literally inhuman.

All stories carry the seeds of inspiration (Joseph Campbell). Therefore their impetus must chafe at the status quo. The Promised Land is a condition; it's the opening, however you re-create it. This must be allowed to prosper in the self. Thus the Promised Land is wherever you are when your soul opens. This promise exists in all of us. However, we will nevertheless need a place where the seeds can be planted, and allowed to flower.

Trudeau said, in 1968, in the speeches he gave to win the Liberal leadership and succeed then Prime Minister Lester B. Pearson, that Canada must become "a just society." His essays in *Federalism and the French Canadians* grappled with the idea in speculative glimpses. While it was a catch phrase, suitable for electoral banners, it was also one of the ideas that pressed upon him, and drove him into a life of public ritual and ceremony, political action and compromise. "A just society" is part of the unfinished business we have with Trudeau, and he with us.

*

Imagine an era where everything is possible, because open.

If the idea of a just society hasn't passed, it is because we still have to understand the destiny of the phrase. It may mean leaving the doors open enough to let us experience what comes next. But if you open the doors even if only a little, then you are obliged (at some point) to go through them, and engage what may be there. An opened door intimates that there will be rooms, and more rooms, spaces beyond the frames. This is the extravagant, often devastating, challenge of anything new.

Justice is also the call to cosmos—not to a universe of smashing particles, random and pointless.

A longing for a just society expresses the yearning, never entirely stamped out, for connectedness—"relationship," in Weil's terms.

A just society embodies the hope that there is a harmony of intentions—what we take to be meaning, or (more crudely) a purpose.

It suggests that one may be lost only if there is something (somewhere) to be found.

A just society would be one that acknowledges that mind, or *noûs*, exists primarily in the person. Society, culture, language, race, history, political institutions, religions, must not dominate. It is the *pneuma*, the fire that should be allowed to rise, falling upwards, towards its source.

The stoics thought *pneuma* was "the vital breath." It was "the force that through the green fuse drives the flower," Dylan Thomas wrote in his poem of the same name. *Pneuma*, both fire and breath, is what creates the deep well in personhood.

Trudeau said in 1959, "The Just Society is the one towards which every citizen must work, and the first condition of such a society is that of respecting the liberty of individuals."

Perhaps we can mark a just time by its preservation of contradictions and vulnerability. It would be when every being's cry is heeded, and each person is read differently.

Yet if everyone is a text or a web of multiple meanings, then readings are potentially infinite. Training in reading is necessary. The writings of the Kabbalah insist that we learn, gradually, how to read the alphabetic letterings of the universe, and between its lines. *The Hermetica* also says that education is a necessity; we read, and are read, by others. Passing from one meaning to another is hard work, and open-ended. Therefore the mark of a just time is patience. Force should be used only when non-violent means appear unsuccessful. A person is a sovereign vessel. This is why there must be unease with collectivities and stringent assertions of authority and borderlines.

Trudeau came to know (from his travels, from his witnessing of events in cultures different from his, from his readings, from his encounters with teachers who lived elsewhere) that a just society must be pluralist. Violence in the name of revolution, whether from the right or the left, will extinguish the myriads of lights headed for a decent world.

A just society will appear less spectacular, and less clearly defined, than a society with totalitarian leadership, theocratic goals.

The paradox is that a just society would welcome the sacred without canonizing the sacred. Canonization of a state, like the canonization of mythic writings (say, the Bible or the Qur'an), could turn citizens towards a robotized condition, ruled (and ruined) by ban and veto. A proscribed society isn't likely to allow anything new. We can be deceived by devotions. The judicious, evolutionary processes of a just society would therefore appear more like an unfolding towards an ever-elusive point, following a script (or a charter) that should never become scripture.

That Trudeau was never able to achieve the goals of a just society shouldn't surprise us. The movement towards justice demands that we patiently live with incompletion. This process insists on an infinite capacity for tolerating many points of view.

A just society, for Trudeau, was not a triumphant Marxist synthesis, the completion of historical progress, the achievement of revolutionary Utopia, a final resolution of all inequities. It was the artful balancing of competing ideas and energies. The balancing would allow the person (and personality) to evolve, to emerge. This was a Thomist perspective, surely, of just proportions, making the system bend towards the encouragement of the higher self.

Here is what he said in 1972, "Because we are mortal and imperfect, it is a task we will never finish; no government or society ever will. But from our honest and ceaseless effort, we will draw strength and inspiration, we will discover new and better values, we will achieve an unprecedented level of human consciousness . . ."

Considering the Rose

1987.

In the lobby of Heenan Blaikie.

"Where are we going for lunch?" Trudeau asked.

He had walked in, almost jauntily, wearing a stylish light suit and tie. I had worn an open shirt, a jacket and jeans.

"Why don't you choose." I evaded my less than precise knowledge of restaurants in Montreal.

"All right. Please wait. I'll be right back."

In a few minutes he returned from his office. It was isolated behind a closed door that led to an arrangement of offices. Again, there was no security apparent. This refusal of protection was, I surmised, a deliberate vulnerability. Possibly the absence of security signified this, I can take care of myself. (Trudeau was much less formidable physically than he appeared on TV. He did, however, have a red belt in karate. The red is one below the black. He hadn't quite mastered that self-defensive discipline; but we can say it was close enough.)

"All right, let's go."

He'd added a red rose to his lapel.

"Why the rose?"

It was a question I'd wanted to ask before. He was rarely without one, usually red.

The ironic smile.

"This one?"

"Just in general."

"You want to know."

"Yes I do."

He still appeared amused.

"For show," he said.

He glanced down at the rose.

"A flash of style. It gets attention. And people talk."

"For show," I repeated.

I was disappointed by his answer.

He looked up suddenly when he heard the tone of my voice.

"Well, it's more than that," he said.

There was a pause. He seemed to be surveying the scene. Then he looked into me. And he shrugged.

"The style is the man, yes?"

He gestured towards the elevator, and we were off.

Observers say that the rose in his lapel was a public relations move. And yet the rose appears in photographs before he became Prime Minister. It's been said that he was told to wear it by advisers, ever aware of his eerie ability to communicate without saying much on TV. (Yet he wore it long before, and continued to wear it long after, the cameras were turned off.) Some claim that they know who gave him the rose. (However, all his biographers step back, and acknowledge that no one truly knows.)

*

Consider the rose.

"The perplexing redness of its red" (Borges).

It is a symbol of completion, and corresponds with the harmony of a circle. Hence the rose links to the sphere, the oldest symbol of the soul. Vivid red is the colour of the heart.

He was observed wearing different shades of roses over the years. They could be yellow, sometimes white. There could be shadings of meaning for different occasions. The actor must know his audience. A white rose conjures mourning, loss, and friendship, unity. A blue rose represents the impossible, a gold rose—achievement and excellence.

The colour he chose most often was red, of course. It was a witty gesture; red is the colour of the federal Liberal Party. It also parallels the red leaf at the centre and the bars at the sides of the Canadian flag.

The story of the rose is steeped in the mythic. It symbolizes identity, the flowering of the self. When a circle rises at the intersection of the cross, we call it the *ankh*. This is the Egyptian cruciform. It means that knowledge swells in the union of two directions, the vertical and horizontal, up and down, the sacred and profane, the hidden (esoteric) and the ceremonial (exoteric). The rising suggests a billowing sail on a ship. It evokes pregnancy. In other words, a vessel fills. These are images of inspiration, and of a virgin birth—new ideas entering into matter. The cruciform and the sphere together are often called the rosy cross, *rosenkreutz*. Turn the *ankh* on its side, and you get a key. That key may fit the doors of perception, opening life to infinity. In *Der Rosenkavalier*, Richard Strauss's opera, from the libretto by poet Hugo von Hofmannsthal, the knight of the rose is a romantic hero offering his services to love when he delivers a rose. Red; colour of passion, of rage. Red is the warning sky at morning, hopeful light at night.

The shadow of the rose haunts literature. The white rose reaches an apogee in Dante's *Divine Comedy*, in *Paradise*, when the empyrean flower revolves, in God's dance, joyful spirits whirling round its rim. This is a vision of the cosmos in harmonious prayer and celebration. The metaphysical rose proves too much for the poet, who turns away, overcome by perfect beauty. He finds himself incapable of finding words for the ineffable. Dante, the most precise of poets, a scrupulous philosopher of craft, stopped at the edge of language. Yet the symbol remains; the rose offered a light that burned, but did not annihilate.

In *Four Quartets*, T.S. Eliot recalls the Dantescan moment. The poet gazes longingly, and nostalgically, in "Little Gidding," into a timeless condition beyond time and place, where the lost unity of heart, soul, mind and matter will be restored, "And the fire and the rose are one."

It will be H.D., in the poems that make up her *Hermetic Definition*, who will ponder how the rose is sexual, the flower of erotic secrets. (And to remind us that in a cosmos of symbols all things are coded and intertwined, the title of the book cryptically carries Hilda Doolittle's own initials.)

Sub rosa means "the meeting is confidential." The rose is the supreme emblem of enigmas.

In the ubiquitous novel *The Da Vinci Code*, Dan Brown is much exercised by rosy implications. The rose becomes a symbol for female genitalia. It represents the concealed generation of ancient bloodlines, and the conspiratorial obfuscation of the sacred feminine in history. Rose lines like menstrual blood on a map of Paris mark significant longitudes.

I doubt if much of this is what Trudeau had in mind when he wore his rose.

"A rose is a rose is a rose," Gertrude Stein said. She meant that we should be careful about making too much of anything.

Yet: "The eye reads omens where it goes/And speaks all the languages the rose" (Emerson). In one more turn of the screw (as it were), the symbol of the rose links with the idea of true direction. A Charter of Rights is an indicator of routes. The rose, with its five-petal circle, is a form of compass. To what does the compass direct us? The gaze is from seed to flower—from a closed and compressed entity to blossoming receptivity, an embrace of existence. The completing part of the compass-rose is the air, what stirs in the invisible current.

The rose is thus a meditation point. One may focus the

mind upon it, intensifying thought. The rose speaks of the heart, and of ideas and references, feelings and passions, that need to be kept close to one's deepest self. "Learned by heart" is a synonym for memorization, the most profound form of learning. There are some things we keep close to our hearts because we are not ready to speak of them.

Trudeau knew that what holds a society together is a *sensus communis*. This is the moral minimum of shared values and longings that allow the individual to seek his or her destiny. Laws (a constitution, a charter) safeguard this process only to a certain extent. The spirit of a country has to be written in that reason which only the heart knows. Threaten the balances of justice and you threaten the potential enlargements of mind and soul. Therefore justice is part of the safeguarding of the heart.

Then again, his rose was "a flash of style."

He was an instinctive actor who loved the camera. Like any celebrity, he knew he was being observed. Whenever we walked into the building lobby, out onto the street, stood at a corner, crossed the street, entered a restaurant, he quickly became the focus of attention. ". . . for the roses/Had the look of flowers that are looked at," Eliot wrote (ruefully?) in "Burnt Norton," the first movement of *Four Quartets*.

Politics was spectacle and buzz. Even friendship could be a spectacle. He knew, perhaps all too well, that I noted what he said. Someday, he must have recognized, I'd expand my notes into larger reflections. These occasions and conversations would be turned into intersections of interpretation.

Questions and Quests

At the crossing, in the crucial time, questions are put to the pilgrim. The unsheltered moment is shattering, rarely solacing. A riddle is posed to wake us up. "To the blind all things are sudden" (McLuhan). The daimon, the voice in the wilderness, the road to Damascus, the dark night of the soul, the wind rustling leaves and rippling water, Federico Garcia Lorca's "black sounds" ("shadowy, palpitating") are metaphors for that instant when something comes, with annunciations and intimations, demanding a reply.

You find yourself at a turning point. What are you supposed to do? Incline an ear, open your eye, apply your mind, imagine more than what you might have perceived in your immediate surroundings.

The inspired moment seems to say, choose; resurrect from your old habits into the new.

The abruptness, even the violence, of the awakening

can be of such intensity that we call it an apocalypse. This is "the lifting of the veil," the tearing of the cloth that obscures insight.

You can close your eyes again (it's certainly an option). Warily, you could just try to avoid the whole thing. The crossing could appear anywhere, at anytime, however. It's likely that it will continue to startle by showing itself like a chasm, an abyss, a flood, a storm, an aperture, until the pilgrim (you) finally responds.

Now we experience apocalypse 24–7–365 with our electronic screens. Spiritual and existential riddles come calling, in the images and sounds we receive.

The e-screens are our crossroads. Identity and electricity are the cruxes we bear, the intersections where we have arrived. The global village is a ritual theatre where everyone watches, and feels they are somehow performing and being watched, recorded in shadow-data files.

And this process is much more: it is a Mystery Initiation, where we are still being asked, like the ancient neophytes poised at the entrance columns of Eleusis, what is the human? . . . or, is this you?

What is the Media Mysterium?

Let us revise and adapt Nietzsche on the ancient Mysteries. When every image speaks as an energy field, when every apparition carries us, seducing us with virulent moods, when presences appear consistently in our lives, when emotions take us, and sometimes break us, into inexplicable epiphanies, when new forms and figures from technology (say, crosscuts and montages) dominate our modes of response, when we feel close to fire and the ungovernable, when images themselves become knowledge (and so they always were), then we operate in multiple worlds, where anything is possible, and everything is present, and we sense that the cosmos itself surrounds and engulfs us, and we find ourselves taking on new shapes of thought and feeling. We are then "threshold crossing" (Joseph Campbell), on the cusp of what seems like other worlds, which are metaphors for crossing into different dimensions of awareness. Once across the threshold of the e-media, you are into the sea—the rolling currents of mythic patterns and symbols. This roll of electronic waves is an echo and reflection of "the roll of the waves in the celestial abyss" (the Qur'an).

The pilgrim is on the quest for transcendence, seeking the sacred, craving light and inspiration. Transcendence implies that the pilgrim must break through the boundaries of his or her social and cultural order.

Immanence says light and inspiration are everywhere. The cosmos is alive with the vibrations, and intimations, of the sacred.

Let us posit that the Media Mysterium is both a subconscious initiation and a global alchemical amphitheatre. We are all hungering pilgrims drawn in, and absorbed, and we are entertained. Every screen is an intersection.

We seek ways beyond our confines, and in the meantime, the e-cosmos is enchantment returning; electricity in-spirits everything.

At the threshold of ritual knowledge, the Eleusinian doorway, the questions were posed by the hierophants, the protective priestesses. Where were you formed? Where will you go after this? What moves you?

These were meant to daunt the pilgrim. They would dislocate his or her attention towards knowing the magnitude of the quest. The pilgrim could choose to withdraw. Beyond the columns of the doorway was the unknown: darkness and descent, rumour, legend. And we see how the Oedipus story, evoking the moment when the Sphinx confronts the pilgrim at a fork in the road, is a dramatic variant of this ritual process.

These questions now bear down relentlessly, in the beams of electricity informing our living rooms and workspaces. We linger at the portals of discovery, only they are screens. They offer spectacular entrances, in the brilliantly lit circuits of the cosmopolis.

The screens have become high-definition and wide, implying expanse and reach, breadth and height. Startled all the time to the point of fatigue, so that we are lulled into thinking nothing unusual is happening, we are sleeping initiate media users. It's a Mystery School without due acknowledgment, without the guides for its hieroglyphs and revelatory ceremonies and magic. Instead of select preparations for acolytes, readied over many years for their Eleusinian descent, the initiations are global, and immediately democratic.

The e-cosmos is the great apparition shining, not so peacefully, around us. While we may sit alone receiving, in our viewing rooms, before our screens, we are not unknown.

And what are we being initiated into? . . . The closeness of all souls, and the nearness of the pulse.

"Everywhere and every age has become here and now," McLuhan said. "History has been abolished by our new media." Each of us has become both the eye that watches from a distance and the "I" that enters. (Anyone taking part in a ritual is both one and other.) Voyeur and voyager are not very far apart in this process, if there is any separation. The borders between public and private get erased, and intimacy and exhibitionism mingle. Over every TV and VDT screen we should insist that these words be emblazoned, like a terrestrial branding, welcoming and warning,

"Watch, and Know Your Self."

*

I first responded to Trudeau through images and through his quick remarks about a just society. Images demand that we fill in information. Aphorisms and synoptic remarks insist that we unpack what is left unstated. If Trudeau thought he was being called to account, if he was indeed being questioned by a higher idea, then so I thought we were being called to respond and to account for ourselves.

He insisted that there was a Canadian crux. Did we wish to become a cosmopolitan model for the emergent global society?

If the idea of a just society was part of what drove Trudeau into politics, then the question he posed evolved from that inspiration, however it came to him. "Who speaks for Canada?" He often asked this during his last turn in the Prime Minister's office (1980–1984). "Who will speak for Canada?" he asked, in a variation on that question.

Inferred in those questions were the probes "Who will speak for the whole? . . . What does it mean to have a destiny? . . . What does it mean to feel that there is more at stake here than a hunger for power? . . . What does it mean to live on an unprecedented, experimental path?"

Others who have entered the Prime Minister's office since Trudeau's departure from it have been less sure about the imperative of the questions. Most have shied away from them. They seem too gripped by needless intensity and extravagant drama. Given the proximity of our empire neighbour, the United States, it is realistic to expect that this delicate position will require prolonged periods of prudent negotiation.

Yet part of Trudeau's allure comes from the master story he told himself, and in the question he pressed upon us: Is there a country here?

This was a portion of what taunted him, spurring him on.

II

PATTERNS, SEEDS, CLOAKING
SOUL CIRCLING

Your spirit and the fire contained within you are drawn
by this nature upward. But they comply with the world's
designs and submit to being mingled here below.

MARCUS AURELIUS

We may come to think that nothing exists but
a stream of souls, that all knowledge is biography,
and with Plotinus that every soul is unique.

WILLLIAM BUTLER YEATS

You keep coming through, Pierre, in the communication waves.

Decades later, after you've passed, in spite of criticism and exposure to denunciation, in spite of analyses and microscopic examinations of your life, your questions remain. Can there be a just society? If so, why not in Canada? John Kenneth Galbraith, one of your teachers at Harvard, and later an informal adviser and friend—an expatriate Canadian himself—said there could be "a good society." Sometimes it seemed that these phrases were interchangeable. Perhaps you sensed that this idea had to be set in our minds so that it could beat and grow louder, like the metronome of the heart, moving us, gradually.

In your strange way you often lived directly in the here and now of what we call the vertical and the horizontal. The collision of these realms is a weird space, located between the idealist calling and the media's stream of appearances, between the historical level of practical involvements and the dreams that tell us we both wander in this life and long for elsewhere. We are half in the domain of ideas and dreams—mythic consciousness where we breathe in the traces of the eternal—and half in the domain of existential choice and failure—the plane of time, the part of us that breathes in the perpetual threats of disillusionment and disappointment. It can be a terrible, and terrifying, pressure living in the grip of those realms. But the horizontal plane also tempers the vertical, bringing (one hopes) humility.

"Mysteries cause men to be humble," you said in 1970.

A just society must be a place where we make a case for cosmos—connectedness and principles. It is where the good life gives each person a moment when they arrive for themselves at a turning point of "mortal questions" (Thomas Nagel). It would make the vertical and horizontal apparent to some, perhaps enough who will move up and down the secret staircase of the spirit, and find their particular inspiration.

Pierre, you continue to stir us to questions. This may be because we haven't found satisfactory responses to the interrogations "Who speaks for Canada?" "What gives us a reason for being here?" "What is a just society?" "How do we make it come about?"

Something of you and in you comes through your erratic beginnings and obscured origins, your warrior pride, your need for privacy, your refusal to allow racial identity or a single language to be the basis of the Canadian state.

Yes, you reappear and revive, deepened by continued readings and viewings, in the intersection of eyes, the apexes and gulfs of our attention.

Readings

1987.

I arrived at his office, bringing books.

In my satchel I'd packed *The Glenn Gould Reader*, Canetti's *The Human Province*, Josef Skvorecky's *The Bass Saxophone*, Italo Calvino's *Invisible Cities*, a small book on the Montreal automatist movement, among others.

"Surely you will let me pay for these." His eyes were wide with surprise.

I refused to let him pay.

"Thank you. I'll read them all . . . with close attention."

I handed him a novel by my father, *The Aberhart Summer*. Its inscription to Trudeau read, "Here is another vision of Canada . . ." I knew he would find the depiction of the rise of the dissident Social Credit movement in Alberta of particular interest. Ernest Manning's Social Credit Party would eventually provide the foundations for Preston Manning's breakaway Reform conservative party. Fathers and sons, I mused.

He flipped the cover over and gazed at the author photo.

"Not much of a resemblance," he said.

He turned the book back to the front cover, and its image of a political rally.

"Why don't you bring him along for lunch sometime."

I said I surely would. (My father never did come. He would meet Trudeau only once, years later, at the book launch for *Towards a Just Society* in Toronto, and then briefly that night, in a crowd.)

"I'll have them read for the next time you come by. We can talk about them over lunch," he said.

Books, I would find, were his constant companions in his retirement. He always had a book on his mostly uncluttered desk. (Why should we be surprised to find a political leader reads? Perhaps it's now a surprise to find that anyone reads by choice.) He told me that he annotated books. He'd find the time to withdraw from engagements, and make notes in margins. (This habit was formed young, John English and the Nemnis report in their biographies.)

Then he told me of his love for poetry, Baudelaire, Lorca, St.-John Perse, Hugo, and how he liked to memorize lines. It was as if this too, with his readings, in later years, was a way of forging an accompaniment in an elliptical mental journeying.

"People say I should write my memoirs. But at the moment I'm not sure I should write anything . . . that conventional. I'm comfortable with shorter forms, especially the polemic. . . . I should give you one of my books while you're here. Have you read *Two Innocents in Red China*?"

I nodded, and said I had, years back.

"And?"

"Not one of your best."

His eyes narrowed. His smile didn't indicate amusement.

"All right." He shrugged. "I'll concede that one."

"Do you have a favourite?" I asked.

"My essay, 'L'ascéstisme en canot.'"

"The Ascetic in a Canoe." (It was published in 1944, a long time ago.)

"It's the one where some poetry came out. I wish I could write poetry. But the essay is the best I can do . . ."

"It's a fine form for describing the moment. It has lots of flexibility."

"Yes, it's best for those moments when everything is clear. And the one place where I could sometimes write from here."

He gestured towards his heart. After a moment he moved on, in the conversation, to other things.

"Here."

He had pointed to his heart. Then in a way I had often witnessed, he hurriedly moved on from such a declaration, or admission.

Here: it's a summoning, a directive, a location, and (possibly) a word for the call. It can be a mere marker on a map ("You are here"), but it also points to the present moment's evanescence. "Here, now," the grail of consciousness; can you find it, and open to the new? Time binds, yet to hold on to a moment is to try to seize the unbound.

"Make it new," so Ezra Pound and H.D.'s Imagist Manifesto urged. This meant, make the moment live and endure, "Quick now, here, now, always." The essay is a form, outside of the lyric, perhaps most appropriate to finding our way towards "here."

And so Trudeau is still here, in these memories. Memory is also a home for images and symbols. Your memory may read and review our experiences, embellishing them, developing them, giving you permission to return in deeper circles of understanding, circumspections that you hope will lead to comprehension.

*

"We have much to discuss whenever you come to Montreal," you said in a letter you wrote to me in 1993.

Our dialogues have become reflections in which I go on considering your gestures and remarks, your evasions, your courtesy, your private and public adherences.

Memories evolve. This is another crucial turn I've discovered when I go back; memories transform the one who remembers, even if one tries to forget or repress them. The past doesn't stay still any more than the present does. We edge closer, living again inside statements and incidents, moving towards those people we have known and admired, and feared and been bewildered by, and they begin to show themselves again (abruptly, often slowly) in the layering that is thinking, remembering, projection, exposure.

History is the steady study and gathering of dates and facts, of motives and actions, from evidence and testimony. We want history to restore the elusiveness of the moment in a satisfying series of logically arranged analyses. We think sequence will solve our mysteries. Yet I keep coming back to cryptic utterances and omissions, Pierre. There are only more readings, and questions that lead to more riddles about identity.

"To rise from history to mystery," Norman O. Brown said in *Closing Time*.

Thus history slips, slides away, alters, won't stay still. It is another type or pattern of the imagination, Frye said. Patterns may become illuminations that unfold into more stories—suddenly exposed trails that ask us to follow to whatever unexpected crossings.

The imagination is the mediating point between the soul and the material world, Frye implied. And the soul has its own communications. We may get at that track through images, moments, the masks of personality, readings and re-readings, and the inevitable fictions that are our stories.

Memory comes in breaks, waves, seeds, bits.

Pierre, when I reflect on these moments, I wonder, did we make ruthless use of one another?

The poet in me was seeking symbols and myths, deeper than history. The politician in you, crafty and manipulative, wanted a story and image to get out. Who was using whom?

> You were capable of rearranging facts, and of omitting details, to suit you. While this raises questions about the nature of truth, I know how you were creating a self, projecting a myth.

Charismatic Fictions

1987.

I saw first-hand his need for fictions. This was also a reflection of his need for irony. Whether it was wearing a cape and a bohemian hat to a football game ("the Mandrake the Magician" costume, so it was dubbed by Canadian Press; he was the dandy descending into a swarm of jocks), or obscuring his real age (he consistently said he was younger than his actual years), or appearing at highly publicized events and saying next to nothing (at the 1985 book launch in Montreal for Jean Chrétien's memoir, *Straight from the Heart*, he was asked for his opinion of the book; he scampered away from pursuing cameras and reporters, and snapped over his shoulder, "Haven't read it yet."), or appearing at small occasions when there were no microphones around and speaking, transfixed and impassioned, of the necessity of Canadians to rise about provincial squabbles (so he did in a town in Alberta, in the failed election attempt of 1978), he recognized that the internal narrative (the daimon call) should appear in masks.

Over lunch in Montreal, in the winter, we talked about

the essay I'd written about him that was soon to appear in a book.

"Given your reticence about explaining yourself to the press, it's inevitable people will ask how we met," I said.

"How did we meet?"

He seemed genuinely curious. (He could be forgetful.)

I offered my version.

"Yes. We must make sure our stories are the same. Just in case someone asks," he said.

I reminded him of the first call, the first visit, and the subsequent calls and visits, after he had invited me back for lunch.

"Well, now. That seems to me as good a version as any. Tell it to me one more time so I can remember it. If anyone asks, then I can refer them back to you."

"This is the version we can agree on."

"By all means. I like how it sounds. Use the stories in any way you see fit. What you've just said is a good version."

Trudeau found delight in surprising or unsettling people. I supposed that by keeping things off-kilter he amazed himself. These were ways of drawing attention too.

"Besides," he mused more to himself than to me, "controversy is good, especially for a young writer. If people find holes in things, then they'll ask questions. Controversy is good for others too. It keeps everyone awake."

*

1992.

His need for irony extended to fellow politicians.

At noon I stepped out of the elevator, into the lobby of Heenan Blaikie, and bumped into Jean Chrétien. We spoke briefly, and I went on to Trudeau's office.

"Did you see Chrétien?"

He nodded towards the doorway as if the leader of the federal Liberals and the Leader of the Opposition were still standing there.

Trudeau had settled into his chair, and sat watching me, while I sat down on the other side of the desk.

I had, I said, at the elevator.

He smiled like the proverbial cat that had just swallowed the canary.

"He likes to come here quite a bit . . . for *advice*."

"Does he need it?"

He shrugged.

"He certainly thinks so."

(However, four years before, in a September phone call, he told me of his desire to stay away from politics.

"I keep trying to stay out of Mulroney and Turner's hair. I wish they'd keep out of mine. I really would like to stay out of things, for now.")

*

1990.

His irony could turn predatory.

At the Calgary Liberal Party Convention—the Chrétien Coronation (so it was called). I had come down from Banff, in the mountains, where I'd been working on a book at the writers' colony. Dennis Mills, then member of Parliament for Toronto-Danforth, had invited me, and I was his guest.

Trudeau almost sprinted out of the Saddledome Stadium guest area where he'd been seated observing, just after Paul Martin's leadership speech. (Martin was one of the few who had unsuccessfully tried to prevent a first-ballot victory for Chrétien.)

We passed by each other in the hallway.

He called my name.

"Did you hear the speech?" he asked.

"I did."

"All that money behind Martin, and they couldn't buy a decent speech writer?"

*

1989.

His savage irony could be turned towards a friend.

"Your French isn't very strong," he said, in his office before we headed off for lunch.

My French wasn't strong. I had some ability to read our second official language, albeit slowly. This far outweighed my ability to speak it. We always conversed in English.

"Do you think that's appropriate, given your . . . beliefs about Canada?"

I winced.

"After all, it's part of what *you* believe . . . being bilingual, and multilingual."

Trudeau had emphasized that learning another language was a gift, not a burden.

I was ashamed of my mostly monolingual capacity. When I went to live in Quebec City for a time (in 1991; it was a year of wandering), I struggled to improve my French, to little avail.

*

1998.

I acknowledged my inadequacies in French during one of our last encounters over lunch.

"Still trying?" This time he was kindly.

"Still trying."

"Well, keep at it."

He gave me a sympathetic look, and then shrugged.

*

1998.

He was damning that day about what he perceived to be racism in English Canada.

"We'll always be fine in any referendum, so long as someone in Ontario doesn't choose to burn or trample on the Quebec flag."

He remained outraged over what he perceived to be Québécois racism.

"When you hear them say [I presumed he meant diehard nationalists] they want to be '*maîtres chez nous*,' does that house include the aboriginals, the Jews, Italian-Canadians, all minorities from around the world, any of the so-called others?"

When he spoke in this way he became clearer in his being. In his ironies I detected the surging of his inner turbulence, his need (always impending) to change others' opinions. Following the inward narrative meant challenging the stories people told themselves.

*

1998.

One more shift into severity.

"And how are your children?" he asked. We were still in his office.

"Fine. Very healthy," I said.

Then I mused out loud on their six-year-old tendency towards stubbornness and wilfulness. "I believe they both have incipient prime-ministerial qualities."

A cutting glare. His eyes slashed at me. His mouth drew tight. He squared his shoulders.

"And what exactly are *those* qualities?"

I almost enumerated: a penchant for self-determination beyond conventional restraint, a taste for autocratic declaration, a sublime self-centredness, the occasional disregard of others' feelings.

This was one of the only times I saw him, during our times together, close to anger.

I changed subjects.

"What have you been reading lately?" I asked.

*

The fire in the soul can be called rage. It can be called charismatic.

Along with "he haunts us still" one of the clichés we assign to Trudeau is the word "charismatic." It is another elusive term that we engage and feel even when we can't say precisely what it is. In celebrity terms it is thought to be aggressive glamour, with an air of edgy destructiveness. The flame of charisma could burn up those who are close by. This fire has the aura of rebelliousness to it, and the burn of disaffection. It could raze those who do not adjust quickly to its intensity.

Heroes and dictators, pop stars and saints—they appear to us radiating an audacious electromagnetism.

But "Charisma is the ability to look like many people at once," McLuhan said. It is the capacity to look familiar—like someone we've met before—and unfamiliar. We may say that the charismatic being is instantly recognizable (because an archetype; a face could carry the look of people we've seen in representations of the past) and original (no one quite looks like that). McLuhan probably meant that charisma is the talent to project a mirror to viewers. We gaze at the fire, and see a portion of ourselves, or how we might like to be.

Charismatic individuals radically conflict with what we take to be the settled plane of reality. They often possess the ability to rearrange their stories in public. Almost at will they re-create their identities. It is a magical ability, we think. We see charisma in terms of power. There is a peculiar radiance and strength in the metamorphic being of those willing to live at their epoch's apogee, on the mythic cusp. They take to heart the Gnostic assertion that each day brings a crucifixion and resurrection.

The metaphysical imperative is at the core of charisma. Most step back from implacable fire, carrying on their lives of quiet desperation. But the e-media beams *kairos* (the demand of the right moment) into our rooms. Epic lives push their fictions into everyday stories through what we absorb from the screens. We are soaked in ions, and the boundless, and we may feel ourselves distracted by exhibitions of glamour (itself a high pitch of energy), or swept away by fluid crises and dreams.

Charisma is a sign of the calling. Saints and pilgrims are defiantly moved by it. This is why a Mother Teresa draws our eyes, and our hopes. Beauty, uncanny photogenic qualities, present in Princess Diana, or in certain members of the Kennedy clan, can also carry the mark of an eerie transcendental energy. The power overflows the frames of the image and the borders of the conventional. Some stars are thus more alive in their images than they are in person. Charismatic energies are signs of inner intensities drawn out into ceremonial and ritual realms.

Shall we say that charisma is the power to weave the mystical with the mundane?

In that abundant energy we perceive enigmas, secretive zones that both invite and exclude. Charisma comes in the moment when vertical information (beauty, imagination, intuition, emotion, the spiritual seeking expression) strikes horizontal experience (the existential, the material) in the person willing to let those forces coincide, or collide.

We recognize charisma instantly, and bask in its seductive charm. It may merely be glitz. But we are apt to be concerned it may rip us into places we don't wish to go.

Hence charismatic beings constantly make up stories for themselves. They are knowing, ironic; larger forces are at work. Each encounter and image opportunity is a possible crucible of meaning, a moment that needs to be seized, and used.

"All media is a fiction," McLuhan said in one of his most penetrating provocations.

"There is no such thing as past history, since it is always a fiction fabricated by the preferences of the present," he probed.

I keep in mind that with a McLuhan aphorism there is never a final resting place of resolved intention. So I take the meanings of these two aphorisms to be this, all communications' artifacts weave spells.

Every telling or presentation will be shaped, according to the medium, the instrument, we use. Book or TV, word or image; each carries a transformative power. The user (him- or herself) is altered by the medium he or she absorbs. We are forever being made and remade by communications. Thus we are involved in a perpetual process of making fictions—myths. All life is poetry. (Was McLuhan adapting Nietzsche's bold declaration that we make the stories we live by?)

We are engaged in the telling and the unfolding of one story, Frye said. That story is about identity. The question constantly put to us by the Sphinx of existence is, Who are you? Identity itself is the process of finding a version of the story that fits you.

In the crossroads of electricity and identity appear the spectacles of mythic lives. Charismatic beings live in the depths and reaches of their quests. Their dreamlike frictions compel us to pay attention. The intensities in their presence may be so powerful that they become hallucinations. They remind us we are living inside these transformations too. The charismatic person will force their fictions upon us, and thereby ask, By what stories do you live?

We may be troubled by the absence of notions of truth in these equations. Wilde's axioms from "The Critic as Artist" are appropriate here: "To arrive at what one really believes, one must speak through lips different from one's own. To know the truth one must imagine myriads of falsehoods." My gloss: we know the truth by comparing the lies. Replace "falsehoods" or "lies" with "fictions," and we enter the realms of mythmaking. Many truths, like many worlds, dance at the end of our pinpoints of awareness.

Let us recognize that among charismatic beings, the mystic and the revolutionary ideologue have deep affinities. Both are joined by a fury at intractable models of reality. To the mystic, this reality is likely to be the body. To the revolutionary, it is likely to be money. Both recognize that there is something poisonous that stains life with corruption. The body, for the mystic, must be disciplined. The rush of capital, for the revolutionary, should be channelled, if not curtailed. Flesh, money; they are not merely material, they are energies, part of the powers that be. The mystic seeks transcendence of the flesh. The revolutionary seeks Utopia, and the division of wealth into the hands of the needy. Both believe that there is another reality somewhere. One calls that reality spirit; the other calls it shared abundance. Neither will comply with what is before them.

This is no doubt why Trudeau and Fidel Castro became friends. In spite of Castro's flagrant violation of Personalism's essential tenet—the right of every person to be—he was a charismatic revolutionary who followed his inner prompting to its existential end. That end was the reformation of Cuba. They were mirror images of one another. Trudeau, however, saw in pluralism and democracy the hope that each person could eventually find his or her unique path, and do so without violence. The imp in him would have quietly appreciated Castro's blatant effrontery to the policies of the American empire.

A just society places tentative boundaries around charismatic beings. It champions many sides. A multitude of stories can exist at once, but none with the claim of lasting authority. The impulses and pursuit of the transcendental would therefore be reserved for the inward domain.

Nevertheless the e-cosmos lavishes into us, startling in its intimations of the immeasurable, in morphing images, everything a link to other links in webbings of unstoppable association. It is an ocean broken up by a myriad of waves. People find themselves rolling on the waves questing, mysteriously floating and sinking, trying to find precarious balance in that mediated space between the social demand for cautious welcome and the ecstasies and paroxysms of information. Thus comes (again) "the medium is the message": we are in the midst of unceasing mutability, in the crucible of effects. This is another possible understanding of what McLuhan may have meant by his most repeated probe.

Trudeau lived out his inward story before the media's eyes and ears. Part of his charisma surely came in his ability to reinvent himself, and then open himself to where the reinventions might lead. He became a soul who lived on the screens of our projections.

Let us return to controversy. Is such mythmaking and fictionalizing a form of lying? Is it a deliberate—and remorseless—rewriting of truths to suit oneself? The questions are moot. I knew Trudeau in his period of withdrawal from most political engagements. He could give free rein to whim. Others who worked with him during his years in power—Jim Coutts, Tom Axworthy, Patrick Gossage, John Roberts—have testified to me that they were not asked to distort facts. Trudeau was, they said, scrupulous with policy and with any information made on behalf of government.

The mythmaking was reserved for his private life and for the persona he adopted for the public drama. In those realms of solitude and ritual, which often intersected, he felt the need to follow his whimsical side, and to follow the dictates of the reason he wasn't going to directly divulge. (We should remind ourselves: we are always making things up. What portion of our lives is spent in imagining and then revising events, in daydreaming and dreaming?) All this, he surely knew, enhanced the aura of mystery. When you are dealing with a charismatic being, driven by inner necessity, then that person must make up his story as he goes.

*

Pierre, you were sometimes discreet in your ways. But you could never be discrete. You were connected to myriads, part of the multiple minds that make up global consciousness.

Still I found at times that in spite of your inward narrative you could be curiously oblivious about your effect on people. Ironies were often directed at others, but seldom at yourself. It was as if your daimon sometimes blinded you to the fact that you were present in people's impressions and memories.

In the years when I knew you, 1985 through to 2000, you (mostly) resisted requests for access. Nevertheless, anyone who knew you could attest to your vexing need for attention. These contradictions and qualities in you do not unite easily in our imaginings. But then I don't think they did for you either. You wrote in a 1939 entry in your journal: "Trudeau? No one knows him. Friend of all; intimate of none."

"Sometimes I think you know me better than I know myself," you said to me in Montreal in 1990. I was too taken aback to ask what you meant. Perhaps it was a reference to a perceived Boswell streak in me. There was that deliberate remoteness in your remark. It was no doubt a gentle rebuke. I now suspect that you were implying, "Don't be too quick to understand."

Yet a charismatic being cries out to be known. And you were X-rayed and taped by lenses and microphones. You became the most photographed, filmed, recorded and debated figure in Canada. You resided in the numinousness of the e-cosmos, that compulsion of epiphanies and synergy of tremors and plentitude that make up the *mysterium tremendum et fascinans* of the new information networks.

Marshall McLuhan was one of your intellectual companions. He often seemed to be commenting on your effect on our consciousness and sensibilities when he said,

> With TV, came the icon, the inclusive image, the inclusive political posture or stance.
>
> At the speed of light political policies and parties yield place to charismatic images.

McLuhan thought there was "an almost mystical link between Trudeau and television" (John English). The screens do not create charisma. They thrive on it.

Yet there were times, Pierre, when the private person you protected appeared at odds with the public persona you cultivated. I was never able to reconcile this in you, given the sophistication with which you dealt with most issues of political engagement and social concern. I sometimes saw gulfs in how your personal life unfolded and your idealist aspirations, and how all this came through in images.

Here is McLuhan again,

> The images of mankind have become the most basic thing about them.

> The sculptural qualities of the image dim down the purely personal identity.

*

1989.

In his office, on Maisonneuve.

"Where is your wife?" Trudeau asked. "Did you bring her along?"

I had done so on another occasion.

"Why isn't she with you?"

He looked at me closely.

"Is everything all right?" His tone was friendly.

"I'm sorry to say we've separated," I admitted.

"Ah." He sat back almost wearily.

We were quiet for a few moments.

"And it looks like we're heading for divorce."

I wasn't sure how much I could say to him. He wasn't keen to hear about illnesses or problems.

"This sounds . . . final," he said softly.

"I think it is."

"You're sure about that?"

"Yes, I am."

He slumped in his chair. Again he was quiet. An air of sorrow came over him.

"I'm very sorry to hear that."

His look was searching.

"You know . . ." He appeared to be considering how much he could say. "I've been through that too."

I almost said, no kidding. Maybe I'd been out of the country when his separation from Margaret had spread in the news like reports of a meltdown at an atomic-power plant.

He went on looking into me, in that searching way. I saw his sympathy. And I was about to speak, painfully, about what had gone on between my wife and me. But I was so amazed by his statement, and the confessional anguish that was in it, that I hesitated.

"Well." He looked away.

After a silence, he said,

"These things usually work themselves out."

His implacable persona snapped back into place. He straightened in his chair.

"I'm sure you know what you're doing. It's probably for the better. These things usually are . . ." he said, in a slight variation of what he'd said before.

The next week he telephoned me where I was staying in Toronto.
"How are you coping? Are you all right?" he asked.
I was all right, I said.
He recommended that I read lots of poetry.
"And Charles Péguy. All this will help."
I was struck then, and I am still, by the concern that was in his voice. Why was I struck by this? Probably I exuded a certain vulnerability, or need, all too obvious at the time, and he was doing his best to be a friend. I was slightly surprised that this public figure, known for his aloofness, would inquire about anyone's state of mind.

*

1988.
We stepped out of the restaurant into a snowfall.
The Montreal streets were suddenly slippery, the sidewalks piled high with drifts. Huddling deep into our coats, we headed off into the storm.
A white-haired woman clutching her coat with one hand and her cane in another tried to make her way out

of a snowbank. She heaved herself forward, and grunted. Stuck, she floundered, calling out.

We stepped towards her. Trudeau moved faster than I did, and offered her his arm. He reached his other hand across to her and guided her to the safer ground of the sidewalk.

The woman stared up blinking into his face.

"I think I know you," she said.

"I'm sure you do." He smiled.

"You look like that awful fellow who defeated that nice Joe Clark," she said in ringing tones. She rapped him briskly on the shoulder with her cane.

"Thank you for your help, sonny," she said.

Taken aback, he laughed. She shuffled off batting snow away with her cane, muttering to herself something about "damn lookalikes." We stood in the pelting storm, looking on while she ambled away.

"You didn't want to tell her you were that man?" I asked.

"Why would I do that?"

He looked genuinely puzzled.

*

1986.

I heard him balk at the conflict that attends charismatic intensities.

A telephone call from Montreal to Toronto.

We focused in our conversation on the essay I'd written on him, and not yet published. I'd sent a courtesy draft in the mail weeks before.

"You're going to call the book . . . what? *The Lone Ranger?*"

"I haven't settled on a title yet."

"Well, it could be something like that."

"*The Deliberate Stranger.*" I was thinking out loud.

"Now about me. One thing here."

Anger surged up in his voice. He isolated a passage from the essay where I'd mentioned that some people had attributed his ambiguous persona, his outrageous and occasionally inexplicable behaviour, to a latent bisexuality. Some said it wasn't so latent.

"Are people still saying that?" His anger was palpable over the airwaves.

I noted that he said "still." Clearly, he knew about these interpretations. (According to John English's biography, *Citizen of the World: The Life of Pierre Elliott Trudeau, Volume One, 1919–1968*, Lester Pearson and Walter Gordon both wondered about his sexual preferences, and asked associates for clarifications about them. The Canadian Intelligence Service, notoriously invasive, had opened a file on him.)

"Some are." I was cautious.

I'd merely identified the controversy in the section he'd singled out.

Ambiguous sexuality is often a mark of charismatic being. Celebrity images can be omnisexual. Electromagnetism itself (AC/DC) is an erotic force. Those who live on screens and in the everyday must contend with attractions and repulsions. Images are always multi-levelled, subject to the wilder interpretations of their receivers.

Sexual ambiguity is part of an evasive otherness. Anyone entirely comfortable with being elusive, with projecting many sides of their persona, must appear divided to those whose minds are divided. Someone comfortable with his male and female sides must discomfort those, of either sex, who are not. We are all well aware that sexuality, like electricity, breaks boundaries.

Then there was Trudeau's fastidiousness with dress. He was mostly impeccable in his appearance. This, at the time, was deemed unusual for a male North American politician. (Would such impeccability be commented on in continental Europe, or in Latin America?) Then there was his physical ease—the result of training in yoga and karate—when many middle-aged men become bloated cripples. There was the showy flair of his intellect. Suspicious too, to some, was his preference for the company of subversives and artists, say, his friendships with Castro and Leonard Cohen, over business leaders and backroom politicians. People sometimes expressed unease over his dedicated single parenting, and his dating of young women; surely he was hiding something, they said. He had decriminalized homosexual acts in 1967 when he was Justice Minister. All this was (possibly) *A Rebours*.

I submit that he was ahead of judgmental stereotypes here. Men would have to learn how to live intensely with their children, not at an alienated remove, and find the mercurial genius to reinvent themselves. If personality must emerge, and prevail, then cultural conditioning and cliché must give way.

Trudeau sometimes flaunted his flamboyance before cameras. (At the Williamsburg, Virginia, conference in May 1983 he attended when he was Prime Minister, he wore a light, tan-coloured suit and fedora in the company of neo-conservatives Ronald Reagan and Margaret Thatcher.) This expressed his resistance to the ordinariness he thought it was his destiny to avoid. His occasional dandyism was contemptuous, a distancing from the smug insularities of political leadership and their businesslike demeanours.

He encouraged complex readings of himself. "Read between the lines!" says the first line of his journal, begun in 1938.

A chilling silence had descended on the phone line.

Then he gave a dismissive snort.

"That's how some see me?"

"Only a few."

"After all this time."

"I don't think it's universal."

He began to settle.

"Well. This will throw them off. It'll mix them up, I suppose."

I wanted to ask him to whom he was referring. The media? His political enemies? The status quo? Moralists and analysts?

"I see it's after five o'clock. I have to be off to meet my sons at home." He became brisk. "Shall we continue this another time?"

"Another lunch."

"Of course." He was cordial once more.

I would return to Montreal for many lunches, but never again to this subject.

Small Town Incident

Others recall Trudeau. Who was this man who was Prime Minister of Canada for fifteen years? What did he address that reminds us of something avid within us? What is it about him that reminded us of the contrary condition that we surmise is Canadian? What is it about his desire to achieve eminence that still unseats us?

We circle around Trudeau. By doing so we make his name and visions a sphere in which we find ourselves processing more than anecdotes and memories; we are inside the shifting patterns of images, the shared symbols of a many-storied country. Memories take on poetic energy, the exigencies of remaking.

We are likely to remember that dealing with Trudeau questions and dares, through the extended nerve-ends of our psyches, brought aggravated moods.

Here is a moment that reveals the grievances left behind by his questioning.

2006, summer in Stouffville. This is the small Ontario town where I've lived for many years.

"Are you writing about Trudeau again?" my neighbour asked. John owned a prosperous small business on Main Street. He was an amiable, generous man, I'd found.

Yes, I said.

"You're putting your other books aside to do it?"

There was an energy gathering in this one, I explained.

"Trudeau's legacy is terribly mixed." He shook his head.

Aren't all legacies mixed? Whose legacy isn't flawed?

This was my neighbour's response:

"Bilingualism is one thing. But multiculturalism has been a disaster. I don't know what a Canadian is now. I don't know what group I'm supposed to belong to. Do new Canadians have any idea? Do they care? There isn't one identity we can call ours anymore. Trudeau did that . . .

"He took us to the edge with his massive ego. Now we have a country where no one is sure what they are. Everyone is a hyphenated Canadian. No one has any bond with what's here. Our traditions go to hell. And what's worse there's no debate about it. Everything is polite discussion. Like we're all a bunch of social workers or something. New Canadians don't care, older Canadians are left out. Trudeau did that. . ."

"You're saying that he has a lot to answer for."

"He does! Multiculturalism makes Canada a synonym for 'sucker.' What other country allows what we allow? Separatists in the House of Commons. Traitors who are eligible for the Canada Pension Plan. Separatists saying we aren't a country. And maybe they're right. Look at it. People allowed to speak their own languages. People who won't assimilate. And we keep changing our national anthem so I can't even keep up with the words anymore. I don't know what my country is supposed to be. Trudeau did this. . ."

Maybe not having one identity was good, I suggested. It was an opening to influences, a place to start rather than end.

He was annoyed.

We stopped talking. Ironically, there was suddenly a polite unspoken agreement between us to avoid the argument. We were going to be civil, and move on.

Identity Probes

. . . In the questions Trudeau posed he knew that identity is not fixed. Genes, the DNA, may be fixed, but not the mind and not the heart. Uncertainty about identity prevents fanaticism. To recognize that hearts and minds are permeable, therefore alterable, is to welcome and acknowledge the stranger.

. . . "The 'stranger' has become the guide; the passenger, the driver" (McLuhan). The cosmopolitan premise insists that walls come down. Then the question of being a citizen of the world becomes one of the most vexing, because who will you be in a society that invites many, and where you are asked to live in the open?

. . . Assimilation is impossible when identity is fluid.

. . . When people talk of assimilation, what do they mean? What should we be assimilated to? . . . British culture? French? . . . to Hong Kong? . . . to Italy? . . . The instant we mention these nations—cultures—we can perhaps picture a political or racial imperative: the cast of a society. But Canada? The process itself is an enigma—myriad, multiform; so Trudeau knew, and lived, in part through the divisions in himself (a francophone father, an

English mother), and through the way he divided himself from his early education and opinions, and embraced cosmopolitanism.

. . . Identity, a task, not a given. At the columned entrances of the Mysteries at Eleusis, the initiate found that the descent, the journey, the quest, and the ascent, must take all of the time in this life, and whatever there was to come.

. . . According to the Gnostics every day is a pilgrimage.

Each day has its own creation (awakening to light, the brightening), its fall into alienation (the feeling of being lost), its exile and wandering (down a street, into an office, into a classroom, back again to one's home), its seeking after wisdom, a searching for prophecy and help (through teachers, guides, advisers, doctors, experts in body and psyche).

Each day has its period of watching and waiting, its crucifixion (a crisis, a Golgotha), its resurrection (revival of spirit and body; a moment of rejuvenation), and its apocalypse (a rising above the mundane to recognize the pattern at play), then its return to darkness (to sleep, to dreams).

Apocalypse is not the end of the universe, and the arrival of a new political and even biological order. It is the end of delusion, when a culture of incoherent pieces becomes a cosmos.

. . . Frye called this process the Great Code. He adapted Blake's proposition that the Bible offered, in its entirety, a metaphoric code of being, a fable of identity outside of history. To Blake and to Frye, the Bible did not report on fact or on the lives of actual personages; if it did, on occasions in its passages, then that was not the point. What mattered was myth, the story of the heart and mind rising to comprehend the soul's code.

. . . The identity quest is to seek sense in what we do, when we wander (feeling adrift), which is, of course, the modern condition, wherever we are.

. . . Infinity terrifies us, Pascal said. So we prefer homes, structures, institutions, security, ceremonies that explain, anything that contains. Limitation becomes equated with duty. And limitation could be exalted over the extraterritorial abyss, where everything crosses and mingles.

. . . Mistakes are spurs. They offer inspirations, incentives to open. The more contradictory one's life track, the more likelihood there is movement.

. . . McLuhan said sovereignty ends in the global amphitheatre. Electricity obliterates borderlines. The world itself becomes an artifact, under the constant surveillance of satellites. There are many realities at once, multiple intersections of the global and local, the cosmic and specific.

Instead of linear explanations and rationales, we find turning points, resonances and reverberations, signs, crossings, thresholds, interfaces of the source (energy) and experience. The web is the metamorphosis of the cosmic opus, where we still carry on interpretations, with endless amendments. Internet is both text and screen, a new spatial dimension.

. . . Pluralism means a respect for worlds within worlds.

What is the evidence for multiple visions coinciding? A room full of Picasso paintings (the supreme openness of his eye); a rose growing beside a weed in my yard; the recognition that in nineteenth-century America, Thoreau, Whitman, Dickinson, Melville, Stowe and Emerson wrote close by to one another, each unique in their imaginative slant; the perception that in twentieth-century Canada, in Toronto, McLuhan and Frye, each with his visionary reveries directed elsewhere, passed by one another on the University of Toronto campus; the silence held at the conductor's discretion at the fading end of Gustav Mahler's Ninth Symphony; the recognition that each raindrop, each snowflake, each wave of the sea, each oak leaf, each blade of grass, each tear, has a different shape from the other, no form has an exact replica anywhere in the universe. The knowledge that many dimensions exist beyond our plane of observation should teach tolerance, hospitality to those worlds.

. . . While biographies of charismatic beings continue to fascinate us (witness the number of biographies of Trudeau that continue to appear), confusions about motives remain. The imagination, the seed, the daimon of inspiration, the driving internal narrative, may carry information not available to factual recitation. Love, we say, comes in a moment, like a revelation. But how do you explain love? Something stays slightly beyond articulation. In larger-than-life people we engage the mystery we carry ourselves, and sometimes deny, to our detriment. Repressing the mystery in us leads to neurosis, and illness (James Hillman).

. . . The global amphitheatre has centres everywhere, (McLuhan). Electricity floods frames in "an envelope of sense and sensibility." In this ritual theatre, we are both initiate and critic, inside descending (and ascending), outside reflecting.

Sovereignty: now truly within, and not in political states, or racial ties, political institutions, or linguistic and cultural conditioning, in religious dogma, or in legal arrangements, which we know to be largely temporary. People know this; and if they do then what follows is self-agency. If they don't know this, then they follow, sometimes intoxicated, or swayed.

. . . Consciousness seeks transcendence; emotions and feelings experience immanence, the energy in all things.

. . . Frye meditating in his *Notebooks and Lectures on The Bible and other Religious Texts*,

> The Delphic oracle urged man to know himself, meaning not an increase of introspective knowledge, but the struggling of consciousness which at the same time apprehends the world more accurately. Dreams are subjective, but maybe a dream fully interpreted would become a vision.

The question—How do you become a citizen of the world?—echoes the ancient mystery quests and their questions. Why are you here? Why weren't you led to the open door right away? What is your aim? This triad of metaphysical probes had, *The Hermetica* says, a trio of responses: because I was lost; because my education takes time; to find the kingdom of the heart, wherever it may be. *The Hermetica* says there were three more possible responses to the more well-known questions, Who are you? . . . From where did you come? . . . Where are going? They were, light; from the light; towards repose. These were not directly helpful, but they were meant to be provocations.

. . . Trudeau reflecting in 1944: "[In a canoe] the mind conforms to that higher wisdom which we call natural philosophy; later, that healthy methodology and acquired humility will be of use in confronting mystical and spiritual questions."

This passage is from the essay excursion he called poetry.

We remind ourselves a canoeist learns quickly that while no river, and no current, is entirely predictable, there are patterns in nature.

"All things participate to some degree in the eternal law" (Thomas Aquinas).

. . . A just society promises to encode tolerance for those views incommensurate with our own—to a point, unless those views are pushed into a violent overthrow of the process that guarantees the right to inward evolutions. Be careful about letting revolution come in brutally exclusive forms that disturb the quests of others.

The Fire

1987.

A telephone call.

"How is the writing coming?" Trudeau asked.

He was referring to the essay that I had begun two years before. It was the work that had moved me to meet him, and that I had hoped would be deepened by the direct encounters with him. It had been published in book form.

I said there were controversies.

"Well, the only way to escape criticism is to do nothing," he said.

(This would be a remark he would make many times, in different circumstances.)

"How old are you?" he asked unexpectedly.

I told him.

"In your early thirties . . ."

There was a pause.

"Why do you ask?" I said.

"When I was your age, I still didn't know where I was going. I mean, I was still looking. I was a lawyer, a teacher, a writer, I was doing many things. But I wasn't sure where it was all going. I knew I was preparing . . . for something. But what? I didn't learn that until well into my forties."

"That was when you entered politics."

There were clicks on the line, but no static, so I knew the connection was intact.

"Well, I'm sorry to hear you've been in the hot seat, taking some flak."

His voice was amiable, but he seemed to be evading the implications of his blunt remarks.

"But it's important to be critical, and to be able to take criticism. It makes a person," he said.

I wanted to hear more about the need to find one's way. People called this "the fire in the belly."

"A subject for another lunch."

He was abrupt, signalling the call was at an end.

This was how he often indicated that he had other things to do.

"I'll let you know when I'm in Montreal again."

"Good. Let my assistant know and she'll set it up."

He broke off.

His calls could be this elliptical. Often I left our conversations with much more to ask him. But the moment came, and went. He was good, however, at leaving things out, and I knew that it was best to wait, for another chance, or opening.

*

"Do the Gods put this ardor in our hearts/Or does each man's desire become his god?" This is Nisus's outburst in Book IX of Virgil's *Aeneid*.

There are many fires.

Plato thought it was the intellectual principle of the cosmos. Eternity's drive was the spark in us yearning for the good. In *The Unwritten Philosophy*, F.M. Cornford said fire was "the energy of life itself, the moving force of the soul; and the soul was defined by Plato as the one thing that has the power of self-motion."

Pascal stitched the word "fire" on the inside of his coat. It was a memorial preserving the instant when he was seared by the inflaming tongue of the sacred. He even dated the moment on the parchment he always carried: Monday, November 23rd 1654. What happened that day (or night)? He never said; there were no words for "the inarticulate language of love" (Evelyn Underhill). But fire for Pascal was prophetic intuition, heart knowledge that scorches through being, in spite of our resistance, and our inability to fully express it.

The alchemists wrote about the heart's heat.

In the mixing bowl of elements, the experiment of life that is our magnum opus, we stir together soul, spirit, matter, experience. The heat that warms this stirring is love. The process leads to purification (catharsis), and eventually to wisdom (paradise). To find this heat we must learn to be lovers of life.

The fire recurs in ancient symbols. We find it in the burning torch of Apollo, in the eternal fires in the temple on the Acropolis, on the staff of Mercury, in the ceramic sparks on the Gorgon's head and on Athena's helmet in the masks placed over the doors of the Eleusinian Mysteries to frighten the initiate. Biblical fires erupt in images of burning bushes and desert pillars.

Pythagoras and Empedocles were captivated by images of a volcano spewing fire from the underworld, rising to lick the stars. This evoked the symbol of spirit towering up from supposedly sealed matter. These were visionaries who imagined burning underground streams, in the underworld. One must descend, and emerge, through trials (of fire).

Gnostics spoke of fire trapped in matter.

The soul was snared in stone. Until the stone was struck, and cracked, the fire remained diminished, at a low burn. Once the stone shattered, the fire could ascend, released to light a path for itself. The stone is a metaphor for our natural propensity for ignorance; the fire here is the Universal Spirit, and it may appear like lightning on a dark path. . . . And the shattering? It could be the sound of your heart breaking.

Promethean fire is the lustre of rebellion. It represents resistance to authority, freedom from slavery. Prometheus himself was a trickster, robbing the secret of fire from the gods, and a martyr, suffering eternal punishment for the theft and the gift he passed on to humanity. He was a spark, willing on the new. A Promethean inspiration is a burning away from preordained orders. Shelley imagined Prometheus joyful in his chains, spiritually and intellectually "unbound."

Blake ironically inverted the notion of the tortures of hell. He saw genius relishing fire. The daimon let the heat of imagination melt the mould of convention. In *The Marriage of Heaven and Hell*, he savagely satirized those who feared the flames of inspiration. It was the Spirit calling, asking each of us to move free of doctrinal restraint.

To the mesmerists of eighteenth-century European courts, the nerve-auras of the body were fiery. This was surely an early recognition of the electromagnetism our blood calls and neural networks radiate. Occultists thought that galvanism, or magnetic energy, was "the invisible all" (Madame Blavatsky). It's likely that this is one of the origins of the attempt to read auras.

To Gaston Bachelard the metaphors of fire are the ones we make to express desire and aspiration.

In McLuhan's mytho-poetics, fire is electricity and light. Pulses of energy illumine the global amphitheatre. Electricity is the source we admit into our lives with escalating emphases through screens, wired and wireless machines. We pump ourselves up with the power of the fire. But electricity is a metaphor for the incommensurate too—for the heightened flow from the source, and its emergence into our being.

The e-screens agitate ions.

And electricity runs counter to "the logic of solids" (Henri Bergson).

Through electricity, the fire in us and the fire that may burn from the Spirits are mirrored in the e-environment.

As we burn so the cosmos burns. In this condition the *pneuma* (in each, in the world) is amplified. The cliché "burning up the airwaves" means that input has been pitched to the point of maximum reception. How much of the fire can we take before we turn into ashes?

I've thought that many McLuhan probes were a howl, a recoiling, a prodding, and an oracular caveat and event. He was profoundly ambivalent about the elemental energy that we trafficked and mainlined. In an original draft of his final book, *Laws of Media*, he likened the electric state to that of "Proteus Unbound." Electromagnetism is the dynamism of life; like the *pneuma*, fiery breath. And now we ride this power as if we were saddled on the back of a writhing snake.

Our lives are switchboards of world-feeling. This reveals itself in signals, flashes, advertisements and icons. Messages crisscross. There is no end to the messaging, and its mystic smuggling in of thresholds.

Yes, there are fires, in us, in our imaginations, in our stories, in the daily bread of energy surging through our e-machines. Media *prana*: who knows where such burnings and turnings will lead?

Return

When I return to considering Trudeau, I think of questions I should have asked him. What was the fire for him? What was it in his exposure to the world through his education and travelling that woke him? I probably never asked these because I didn't know how to put them. It takes a long time for some people to know what the truest questions are. Perhaps the call is meant to sear in ways that only one person can truly know. A fire will unexpectedly leap from place to place. Electrons also make unpredictable jumps.

Burn yourself away from origins . . .

The result will be discontinuous. It's the radical leap of faith, elsewhere. This is the uprooting that Simone Weil invoked. "Except the seed die," she said. "It has to die in order to liberate the energy it bears within it so that with this energy new forms may be developed." Once again, roots and aims may not be the same. But there would have to be the intelligent trust that once you tore yourself away, you would fall upwards towards light (which is supposed to be always there), and not downwards, into darkness.

Trudeau's visionary fire briefly became the call for tolerance and justice. The place he elected to live out this intelligible drama was Canada. What is tolerance? . . . A welcome to all who are not like you. Canada was a crucible where the good life seemed possible. Such a seeming still offers a powerful allure.

There was a time when we went along with his idea of the cosmopolis. The person may pass. The challenge may be obscured. Other situations emerge. New people speak. But an idea, like a dream, is a living event, a vibration, a breath, an invitation, an intention, a call in itself for realization. Its energy traces on, rising again with the shift in waves.

Returning to Trudeau I remember how the idea of Canada came to haunt him. It was more than a political arrangement to be defined in only legalistic terms. He knew that we hadn't mirrored or imitated other countries in the world, we'd added to it. This was why the world would come to look towards us, not as a mirror, but as a lamp.

Let us speculate, and imagine:

Trudeau merged Mounier's Personalism with Teilhard de Chardin's noosphere. (Teilhard's books were forbidden publication by the Vatican until the 1960s. But his ideas were in circulation in Paris, and in Catholic intellectual circles.) How does one reconcile the exaltation of personality with dawning planetary consciousness? One path sounds selfish; the other sounds collectivist. We know Trudeau's unease with racial and linguistic collective demands. But we recognize he wasn't at ease with marketplace individualism either.

It was necessary for every individual to develop a personality, according to Mounier, and (intriguing synchronicity) to Tielhard de Chardin in *The Phenomenon of Man*. "Personal development" was essential—in fact, a right. The person must be appealed to through persuasion (communications), and not be coerced into being. The force of collectivity had to be tempered by a Charter of Humanity.

And yet we are evolving into "a super-mind," or "a super-soul," in the wiring of the cosmopolis. The world is a thinking-feeling envelope, becoming warmer because of psychic intensity. (The threat of global warming through pollution is the poisoned, dark mirror of the heating of consciousness into spiritual energy.) In *The Future of Man*, Teilhard asks, "How is this warming of hearts to be realized?" He responds, through "affinities," "nearness," "psychic congregation," "an intensification of reflective life." The global mind is a single spirit in search of itself. In the channels of electricity we find the universal attraction of souls. The personal expands to discover kinship. "Communications is a liberation of consciousness," Teilhard said, in poetic ecstasy.

Trudeau would have instantly understood when he encountered these philosophies that the personal would not be annihilated in this union. When we learn to commune with our whole hearts and minds upon the globe, the world becomes our resting place, where we become still. Each personality is like the expanding sphere of a satellite's wings; or, in the yoga training that Trudeau himself practised (another part of his education in the East), like a tree unfurling, reaching out to receive. The spinal column is an antenna. Personality should vibrate to pitched frequencies, and rise. A person is the hub of the world. And yet each of us, in his or her way, seeks the global face. These recognitions were surely more mystical than ideological.

A just society would implicitly recognize that the earth isn't a meaningless prison, but an emerging call. There are no fixed borderlines in the cosmopolis, only resonances, cusps, centres, intuitions, intimations.

And we see how Trudeau powerfully gravitated towards McLuhan's vision. His myth of the planetary culture "resonant with tribal drums" implied that the world was evolving into the heartbeat of consciousness, "the coiling of complexity." The global village is Teilhard's "superhominization" and "planetization" reborn. McLuhan's insistence on the bedrock of the personal was an echo of Mounier. Separatism was therefore viciously regressive, a retreating into isolated groups, only to be achieved through the purgation of others and bloodletting.

This awakening consciousness would also spell a faith in the future.

The wiring of the consciousness pulse is inflaming. "Eternity is in love with the productions of time," Blake said in his "Proverbs of Hell." By which he surely meant that through our productions and re-creations the cosmos deepens in its teeming. The e-cosmos is the crux of the mundane with electricity, and thus a meshing of the visible with the invisible source. The productions of our time, our e-technologies, are in love with infinity, to revise Blake's hell-forged aphorism.

Trudeau's visionary yoking of Personalism and cosmopolitanism found its fruition in Canada. It could be a channel, a convergence of options. All countries are, and should be, temporary arrangements. ". . . The very idea of the nation-state is absurd," he wrote in 1962. Yet his stormy opposition to separatism came from his inspiration that Canada could become a paradigm for the open society. He sheared away, in part, from his background to meet the energies that emanated into this northern place. Here: don't let the provincial or the conventional triumph; allow us to have our time of adventurous mind. Sympathy would one day be greater than cold-bloodedness. Through the pulse, the world would speak to us, and teach us, day after day, night after night.

*

These recognitions were certainly quixotic. But every dreamer is a romancer of the new. The greatest parable of this is the old Urbina soldier's invention, Don Quixote de la Mancha. In Cervantes' comic quest all of Spain eventually comes to participate in the knight's magic gaze, his obsessed pursuit of an idea. His enchanted eye warmed others (even his sarcastic aide, Sancho Panza), inspiring them. The impressionable Don, however, would think himself defeated, and retire to become a solitary shepherd. The parable tells us we will always come upon dreamers who sees things we don't, and yet their dreams add to the world, enlarging our imaginative spaces with more meaning.

Yet what of the quixotic pilgrim? What becomes of him or her?

The fire of inspiration can bring agencies of daring, and it can bring wounding and loss.

On November 13, 1998, Trudeau's son Michel ("Mike") drowned in a hiking accident, in the icy waters of Kokanee Lake, in British Columbia. Hurt and baffled, Trudeau sought solace in his faith. The once fierce anti-cleric—who nevertheless devoutly attended church—was torn apart by doubt. Liturgy might help. The strict enclosures of the Church could offer solace. He would delve deeper into readings of the Bible. Perhaps to soothe his sorrow he could return to obedience.

Suffering rips us away from roots. Grief shreds the present, and sends us whirling. It takes us, in shock, into a world beyond—the place of pain.

Dogma places limits on the spread of agony. Grieving can eat its way through being like a ravenous disease mercilessly gnawing towards the heart. Obligation, hierarchy, authority, the barricade of tradition, can provide an order for what is tearing up our insides. The bruised pilgrim, accustomed to imaginative exile, could crave a home, a rock. Such a return is surely a shift away from the personal quest to the settled path, and a turning to those who will do the knowing for us.

To be spiritual means to be a lifted spirit, to be inspirited. Make your own script, and don't be bound to scripture. *Religere* is the origin of the word "religious," and it means to bind, to root. It refers, precisely, to being bound in a book.

He had been humbled. The binding he sought was consoling. It was whatever would help to explain to him what was utterly, finally, inexplicable: the death of his child.

So the cosmos of action churns.

"You could not discover the limits of the soul, even if you travelled every road to do so; such is the depth of its meaning," Heraclitus said.

To Heraclitus the soul is an exhalation. It is also both fire and water. We cannot take hold of fire, or water. Surely this is another way of saying that understanding destinies is infinitely complicated. I'm continually confronted by abysses, what we mean when we say "personality," "cosmos," "soul," "calling," "consciousness," "being."

"The soul is a circle," Plotinus said. Circling is an image of reflection, and of return. Every turning must bring a startling revision; and so patterns never stay the same.

*

Pierre, there was a price to be paid for your visionary provocations.

What is a visionary? Anyone who can see a future, anyone who sees that present seeds will yield a future. This imperative proposes that thought is an event. Thought itself is a provocation. *Provocatere*: it means to ask the voice to rise, to bring the voice forward. Every original idea is "in the beginning."

Some visionaries will themselves into receptivity to vertical information. Open the borders, open the senses. Let the other side infiltrate, sideswipe, dislocate, permeate, influence, assist, amaze. Admit it like music. But can one handle the infusions of Spirit? Will it utterly destroy the old foundations? One may invite visionary experience, and then regret it. Can one absorb the flow of imaginative, spiritual knowledge without being wounded? Receptivity takes courage. One must strive to find calm. It takes a long time to learn how to rise up and absorb the sun.

Rages enter; but how do they leave?

Pierre, to you we had in our grasp an original opportunity. Canada itself was a calling. Quebec was inside the process; the other provinces would share their wealth; there would be a legacy of rights; and the aspirations of the cosmopolitan society.

All this carried metaphysical urgency. Such a dimension to one's thoughts brings sublimity—eminence, awe. But it also brings an enlarged capacity for pain and suffering. It can bring peaks and chasms, and the feeling of being left unsheltered.

Most people feel called in some way or other. This may show itself in the longing to be a better citizen, to be a good neighbour, to find a worthy career, to be good partners or parents, to be originators of a business, or a new way of life. This is why we feel that fascination with people who ask us to burn ourselves into new being.

"Ask yourself first of all whether you are kernel or husk," Goethe said. And would we one day, in the quixotic dreaming that is wide awake, start moving towards the implications of making enlightenment a right for every person?

Pierre, I would see the cost of vision in our final encounters.

III

FORMS, EULOGIES
IMAGES AND SYMBOLS

When our guides and those who are cherished by us leave
and disappear, they are not annihilated, they are like
stars that vanish into the light of the sun of reality.

RUMI

He was kind and powerful.
He asked me to read him
a poem. And then he asked
me for another. And another.

LEONARD COHEN

Taciturn Mask, Elusive I

1997.

"At what point do you become enigmatic?"

Trudeau's smile was tight, Asiatic (Attic?), at once mildly mocking and once more amused at the complexities of life.

"Why do you ask?" he said.

I didn't answer immediately.

"Why are you thinking about that?" He spoke slowly. It was, after all, a strange and no doubt self-indulgent question.

I'd observed how his speech had begun to slow down. But he was an elder then, in his late seventies.

"I've been referred to as 'almost' enigmatic in a newspaper," I said. (The newspaper was the *Edmonton Journal*. The author of the article was Charlie Mandel, son of the poet Eli Mandel.) "Sometimes I puzzle over it. When do you go from 'almost' to 'completely'?"

Those words cried out for quotation marks.

Silence.

Laser-blue staring across the table. The smile lingering.

He was probably thinking, Why am I being asked this presumptuous question?

His Jesuit training, and leanings, would have taught him that there were always meanings within meanings. The world imprinted and racked us with significance. Words were themselves worlds. There were questions latent in other questions. Every statement is a premise. The book of the world, *Liber Mundi*, leads to more debate and questions, more dialogues and reflections, an infinity of extensions and correspondences. It could lead to an infinity of misreadings and misunderstandings too. (Let's evolve the metaphor: every electronic web enlaces into a larger search, in a constellation of sites.)

Finally the shrug, and a reply,

"Just stick around."

"Stick around?"

"Longevity. The longer you're at it, the more of a mystery you'll be."

"Survival. That's the key?"

"Just staying alive in this business is part of the mystery. For most people, anyway. Or so it seems."

The smile returned, and didn't fade. Nor did his blue stare falter.

Another silence.

Trudeau's answer, naturally enough, had been more elusive than revealing.

*

Mystic Trudeau / 129

Time: May, the Canadian spring, late as usual, in Montreal, one month before the federal election. The place: his office on the twenty-fifth floor of 1250 René Lévesque Boulevard. Historians with a developed taste for ironic patterns and puckish synchronicities would in the future no doubt take note of that address and street name.

Day: Wednesday, the wind carrying traces of ice; a blue light, a subtle aurora in the sky. Me: taking a break from a round of interviews and readings. Trudeau: thirteen years out of power, deep in his implacable retirement. Yet for many people his resolute remove, the persona of this former Prime Minister, had become ever more impenetrably gnomic.

I'd come for lunch, and I'd come with new questions. It was hard to visit a person in the process of becoming a myth without having things to ask.

And though he was on that day courteous, receptive, almost serene, and certainly articulate, I had the sense of him being turned inward, more so than on those other occasions when we had met. There was a new intensity of inwardness about him. Perhaps I simply hadn't noticed this before. But there it was; a profound sense in him of retreat.

Daydreamy, or contemplative? I wondered. Or maybe a person all too aware of endings, of life's narrowing?

At any rate, he wore a blue suit—more formal than some of the times when we'd met before.

His mood was unhurried, and I felt that way too. We were willing to let our conversation wander. I remained seated in front of his desk, where he was seated, and we talked, in a leisurely fashion, of mutual acquaintances, trips we'd taken and, inevitably, books and poetry. He zeroed in on Yeats and Rilke, two poets he said he was reading closely.

"Their later poems especially. Do you know them?" His question seemed like a demand.

"Yes, I do."

Unexpectedly, as if to test me, he quoted a section from Yeats's "The Second Coming."

"'Turning and turning in the widening gyre . . . The falcon cannot hear the falconer.'" He was almost chanting.

They were apocalyptic lines to be quoting. He went on, stopping suddenly after the first stanza, with its withering aphorism. "'The best lack all conviction, while the worst . . . Are full of passionate intensity.'"

I had the impression I was being challenged. Could I remember or recite what came next? They were lines from Yeats's mid-career that, luckily, I knew, so I obliged.

"'Surely some revelation is at hand . . . Surely the Second Coming is at hand.'" I recited from where he had stopped.

Before I arrived at the passionate arching query to disturbed time that crowns the poem, he broke in.

"'And what rough beast, its hour come round at last . . . Slouches towards Bethlehem to be born?'" He laughed quietly to himself, observing a private joke of some kind.

I thought of how many citizens had sometimes seen him as monstrous before the soft-focus of nostalgia had descended like a haloing mist.

The Sphinx-like beast of Yeats's lines meant many things at once: literal, allegoric, ironic, symbolic or prophetic. Symbolic meaning is fluid, unfixed. One enters the boundlessness of prodigious associations. Such immensity can resemble a glimpse into the abyss, giving vertigo. These lines intimated coming chaos, the start of a new turbulent cycle, where history and myth merge. The poem was launched, almost detonated, by an image of escalation, the falcon spiralling upwards away from a centre. There were enlarging circles, spheres of influence—perhaps images of the soul. Was the soul in the poem being stretched to a breaking point? Was it widening and turning to become a greater dynamo, winding up to absorb more? The rising concentric circles were also an image of increasing intricacies, like a DNA spiral of recombining complexity. Possibly one could read the lines to reveal a coming apex of consciousness. The broadening could move us towards the freedom to fall upwards, into the open, or into the whirlwind.

Trudeau gazed at me then looked off to a point somewhere outside the wide long windows of his office. Then a smile appeared faintly, that private amusement gradually turning back into a reflective look.

"Well, how did you know that one?" he asked, almost with satisfaction.

I told him how I'd memorized poems to help keep me company. (There were other reasons, but that one seemed the best to mention.)

He nodded, as if he knew exactly what I meant. And went silent.

*

I studied his office. It had a measured warmth: large, angular, a bright view of the new hockey arena to the south, a clear aerial view to the east of the park between Peel and Cathedrale, where the rally for Canada took place during the 1995 referendum in Quebec on separation.

Books were stored precariously on top of other books. The stockpile threatened to teeter over in some personal Tower of Babel. I noted the haphazardness of the collection. This was surprising for one I knew to be orderly, at times like a fastidious monk. I glanced over the titles. There were manuscripts and special reading copies among the published books. The subjects were theology, philosophy, poetry, politics, history, memoirs. I saw few works of fiction, another surprise. "Old men read few novels," George Steiner said. Why? Because reality and the worlds of spirit and imagination have fused for a person who had lived with vehemence and keenness? Perhaps at a certain point your internal story becomes vivid enough.

His office seemed as removed as he himself had been for several years. No computer, no fax, no cellular, no typewriter, no TV, no gadgets of any kind. Pens and notepads only.

Pictures of his boys; photographs, and a painting, of the four together. Awards, medals, plaques, testimonials.

"This is where you stood during the rally of 1995?" I asked.

He rose with a sort of sigh from his cushioned chair and walked slowly to the window.

"Yes, from here. I looked down with some others that day at the people, the flags. I could see it all."

"You weren't asked to speak."

Note to myself: I was being too inquisitorial. Did most encounters with him turn into interviews? People wanting to ask things, wanting to know, looking for a way inside, looking for answers.

"No, I wasn't asked."

"You weren't asked to just show up?"

He looked off then down into the park again. That turning inward, that look that seemed to vaguely indicate he was waiting, or searching, for something.

Looking down from this spot in his office one could see the statue of Sir John A. Macdonald. When I'd passed the statue earlier, in the morning, on my way to Trudeau's office, I'd paused to stare at the patch of graffiti, the white-painted smudge, streaked across the cenotaph's base. FLQ, the letters had shouted.

"No," he said at last. "The organizers felt they didn't need me. These strategists had other . . . concerns." Strong emphasis on the word "organizers"; implications of anger.

"It was their show. They thought they knew what they were doing. What they really wanted to accomplish," he said.

"And with the referendum."

"It was poorly handled. No backup plan. Looked like desperation at the end. Which I suppose it was. Giving everything away like that."

"It's quite an image. You standing up here, looking down at the flags, the celebration, the speakers, the crowds."

He turned away from the window, and made a gesture with his right hand, like a farewell.

"I didn't stay here for long. I went out to lunch with friends. I walked in the *other* direction." His emphasis was precise, his intentions clear. "It was cold," he went on quietly. "I had a long lunch."

Quiet. While he'd been talking I'd kept trying to feel the mood of this room. Then it dawned on me: the mood was uncannily quiet. I was tempted to say quietist. An absorption in contemplation, some surrendering to interior life. Despite flashes of wit, and anger, there was calm in him, a deliberate unfastening from the affairs outside. His office located at the end of a long corridor. No one else nearby, except for his polite, discreet assistant, Michele Sansoucy. An office at the edge of a tower. Quiet in the way that signalled be careful about disturbing the peace. Quiet in the way that also said, I'm thinking about things here. The carpeted corridors, the assistants in separated booths. A place not quite part of anything directly. One had to walk up stairs, find one's path down corridors, then find oneself in a place which was, while friendly enough, almost untraceable.

Turning to leave for lunch.

(He: "Will I need my coat?" I: "You will. It's cold out there." He: "Still? It *is* May." I: "I know. But it's Canada." He: "Did I need reminding?")

We went out into the tower's lobby, then into the streaming street, the sudden shout and wind of crowds and traffic.

*

Our conversation shifted to talk of our children. Mine were twins, a girl and a boy, still very young. His boys were now young adults, so he was remembering his experiences of early childhood. (His daughter, Sarah, was being raised in Toronto by her mother, Deborah Coyne.) I had the impression that, chameleon-like, our exchanges were taking on the quality of our environment. Here we were among people talking—couples, groups, trios, soloists, all heading somewhere for lunch—and we had modulated into talk of connection.

We talked of reading to our children at night before sleep, and of learning how to be fathers. And we talked of watching children grow, and of missing them when one travels. We both remarked on how the scent of one's children, and their touch, lingered and sharpened the longing to return home. And we talked of the questions children often ask, of the pleasure and difficulty of getting to know what it is they dream of and what it is they want.

"When they were around ten, eleven, thirteen," he said, "every Saturday night I'd try to get away from my commitments and read to them. It was our Saturday night together. I read them Rousseau, history books, Victor Hugo, and later Stendhal and Tolstoy. We'd talk about what we read. We'd read out loud to each other. Every Saturday night for years. It was . . . one of the happiest periods of my life."

He made it seem like this happiness was in the very distant past.

"It doesn't sound like you've raised your children to be politicians."

"It would be better if they were teachers. Or writers."

"No money in that." I aimed for humour.

"No, but there's a great need for people who can truly teach. Now more than ever. With all the new technologies around . . . I like to help my kids with their studies. Read what they're reading."

Walking on he said,

"Now that you're divorced and your children are spending time going back and forth between houses—something we did too—I'd meant to ask you, when the children are with you, who cooks for them? Who cleans up the house? Who drives them to school, and who picks them up?"

"I do."

He looked bewildered.

"You know, I never had to do any of that."

Startled, I glanced over, thinking: he's being witty. He had been Prime Minister at the time when his divorce was raw. He had servants, cooks, a driver, a nanny. But his head was bowed, and he was staring at the ground. He was walking slowly, and he appeared to be reflecting.

We stopped to cross René Lévesque. Waited for the lights to change. And waited. And waited. Waited longer than I expected he would. A decade before, I'd watched Trudeau sprint off into traffic ("Well, I guess we're off," he called over his shoulder), running against the light, jogging ahead and halting cars, vans, trucks and cabs, with drivers mouthing his name in a pantomime of surprise when they recognized who was dodging through, dashing to the other side, leaving me stranded while the cars picked up speed again. That day he ambled out when the lights finally changed, and I slowed my pace to stay beside him.

*

We were heading for the Chinese restaurant, the Chrysanthemum.

People emerged from towers, rushing off to lunches and meetings, people leaning into the wind clutching spring coats to their necks, people out sidestepping others on the narrow sidewalks, people suddenly struck with that recognition that here was a well-known face passing them by, a face with scars and curves and gashes and prominent bones, so familiar to most that (amazed) they paused to say something to mark the moment, most perhaps gathering thoughts of what to say over a meal, on the way home, in a car or on a bus, in the evening at a café or in a bar, to colleague or spouse or date or parent or child or friend, some registering doubt in their faces—was it a ghost? an eerie simulacrum?—perhaps shocked at his aged appearance, people roaming off to liaisons and appointments, passing by a part of their history, each with a memory of that history—Trudeamania in 1968; the War Measures Act in October 1970; the election defeat of 1979; the election victory of 1980; the referendum battle with René Lévesque in 1980; the patriation of the Constitution in 1982; the polemical skirmishes with Lucien Bouchard—people passing and showing astonishment, sometimes a touch of skepticism and even annoyance, because myth and time and unpredictability and a human presence had crossed.

"Do you ever miss it?"

"Miss what?"

"Do you miss being Prime Minister?"

"No."

"Not at all?"

"Not in any way."

I inclined my head towards him to pick up the words that strayed away, almost lost in the street noise.

"What about the exercise of power? Dealing with issues, with people. Finding solutions or compromises. Finding ways to bring about justice."

The word "justice" seemed to arrest him.

"The just society." He spoke softly again, maybe answering more for himself than for me.

"Being in politics was a role I thought was necessary," he said, "and that I was content to play for a time. Now I'm content to play another role. To be away from it all. You have no idea. I miss nothing."

I was surprised by the weariness in his voice. And I was tempted to intervene in his mood, and ask him what role he thought he was playing now. But I let the moment pass.

We walked up steps to the doors of the Chrysanthemum and entered, found a table, sat down, ordered two plates (shrimp, chicken, with a bowl of hot-and-sour soup for me), and resumed our conversation.

He asked me what I thought of the rise of neo-conservative movements in Canada and the United States. I offered my opinion, and said,

"I believe the neo-conservatives in Canada are more moderate than their counterparts in the United States."

"Maybe." He looked skeptical. "And maybe they're just better at hiding their beliefs than the Americans."

I noted, later in our talk, to what degree he identified any belligerent strain of nationalism with rabid tribalism or racism, and how much he feared the encoding of tribal rights (ethnic rights) into our Constitution. While he applauded the debate of these issues through political symposia, he thought the encoding of such rights would be "a formula for tyranny."

"Any absolute elevation of collective rights—language rights, provincial rights, tribal rights, government rights, corporation rights—over the individual strikes me as being a recipe for disaster. We have to keep watch."

"It should be a tension, maybe a perpetual friction, between the individual and the collective?"

"In a liberal democracy, always. A balancing of rights. Too much liberty for the individual leads to selfishness and anarchy. Too much power for the collective, for institutions, leads to an intrusive statism."

His form of Canadianism—once more: a quixotic cosmopolitanism.

"Yes, contrary to what Samuel Johnson said, patriotism is usually the *first* refuge of a scoundrel, and not the last. Yet one should have a strong feel for where you are. You should be capable of seeing your own time and place."

We shifted subjects, back to books.

He told me he'd been reading the Bible.

"The Bible?"

"I'm reading through it carefully. From Genesis to Revelation. And I'm reading it all . . . slowly. Studying different translations to see how certain words have been changed. I find it fascinating, this question of translation. The differences in interpretation. The mistakes that were sometimes made over the translation of one word. . . . I find the Book of Job particularly interesting these days."

I noticed the preferences in his readings. They seemed centred in works that had formed him when he was young. He mentioned few of the contemporary authors that we had once talked about (and he didn't ask for another list of books). This was another change. Though he was certainly present-minded in our talk, I still had the sense, nothing I could pinpoint, that there were signs in him of a retreat into contemplation. His words carried levels, invoking inner concerns.

People in the restaurant sometimes surged towards him.

I saw looks of hope, eagerness, irony, bewilderment, regret. A sneer here, a gaze of blunt fear there. Words passed; greetings.

He made a brief affectionate reference to his daughter. Again, he became lost in thought.

"And your divorce? Things are settling?" he asked.

"Yes, I'll be fine. But you know, now and then I find myself blanking out. It's as if my mind is in one place, thinking of my children, about all we've been through, and my body and my mouth are somewhere else. It's a strange feeling of disconnection."

He nodded, intimating knowledge of the experience.

"I know what you mean. I lost an entire election in that state of mind."

It was a considerable confession. He looked directly at me. His eyes often burrowed into you when he allowed you entry into his private thoughts. It was a probing look that asked could you be trusted?

"I still miss the idea of a family. It's something that doesn't go away."

He glanced past me as if he was again searching for some presence or sign beyond the table and his company.

The moment passed, the entry point closed.

Back to books, and to ideas about society. He described his recent interest in the legends of Faust (Faust! . . . I said to myself), listing the great works by Marlowe and Goethe on the obsessed scholar who sold his soul to know more, to do more, thus giving in to his craving for absolute power. He talked of "the redistribution of wealth," that apparently taboo idea, banished for years by hardened political moods of remorseless self-interest. Fair distribution, a charter of rights for citizens: these were the touchstones of his dream of a just society.

He'd said that phrase again. There, I realized, was the crucial declaration, the acknowledgment of his heart. Despite what he said about not missing politics, the vision of justice still moved him.

He paid our bill (he always did), and we stepped back into the street.

A last exchange in the law-office lobby.

"Chrétien will no doubt win this election. But by a reduced majority, I think."

"Chrétien. He's a survivor. But I'm not following all that closely," he said.

I turned, getting ready to go.

"I'm retired," he said flatly. He'd added this—for my benefit, or to remind himself? Translation: stop asking for punditry. I smiled at the ambiguities. The statement had several interpretations, depending on how you stressed each word.

Here are glimpses: Trudeau shaking my hand to say goodbye. Wishing me well with my "charges," he said, referring to my children. Saying come back, thank you for the talk. He turned and walked up the staircase. There was no bounding up steps, or *Till Eulenspiegel* antics. But there were no cameras around either. The only ones there to watch were receptionists and fellow lawyers, and they were clearly accustomed to his arrivals and departures. My last thought on that afternoon: he was a person more and more eager to disappear off the public stage.

*

The taxi driver said, "Politics. People like to talk. With the election. Chrétien, Charest. They come and go. I remember Trudeau best."

"Why?" I asked.

The name card taped to the back seat said Angelo. An older man, in his late sixties, I guessed. A heavy accent, broad gestures. Angelo steered his cab through the maul and mew of traffic, whisking me off to Dorval and an early flight home.

"Trudeau? Never had him in my cab. But there's no one like him now. And you know what? He was true to himself. Sure, he made mistakes. Plenty. But so do we all, right? He was different. Made us think. When I first came to Canada, I thought about him a lot. What he was saying about being here. But I never met him."

I told him I had, and that I'd just had a long lunch with Trudeau. Angelo shot me a look over his shoulder, then nearly jerked his cab off the road. I told him it was the truth. He wanted details.

"What's he like now?"

I described a milder Trudeau than the one I'd met in other years. Lucid, aware, attentive, kindly, and yet—here came that word again—withdrawn. I'd found what I thought was a reflective man, gazing into spaces few could enter or fathom. There had been something elegiac in his speech and manner. In his inwardness I'd detected that growing apartness.

I'd wanted to say to Angelo that we were still largely in the grip of Trudeau's idea of country. No principle or idea, narrative, image, symbol or myth had fully succeeded his dream.

And I'd wanted to say that my concern with him was less about practical politics. The imaginative, literary dimensions of his life had come to concern me, and then the images of that life playing through the symbols and moods of the e-media. I was drawn to encounters with the spirit of identity, and its shifts and turns, in the radiating magic of screens. We were encountering lives and appearances, our hearts and minds, and we were watching and colliding with their interventions and evolution.

I'd found a complex soul and spirit in Trudeau. But I'd also found him absorbed by loner reveries. He had seen a great deal. Perhaps enough was enough. When the imagination and spirit begin to wear out because the need to transform realities will leave the dreamer exhausted, maybe then the person will turn to introspection, and the contemplation of loves and losses.

"Never his kind again," Angelo said.

Some might say this is good. The dream of changing the world, and of heeding the call to inspiration, can be too much for many people. The mood in politics has become bruised, overwhelmed, and not transfiguring and transcendental. Perhaps the concerns of country and identity will pass too. Though in the mingling of amped circuits and incited being there will come warmer selves to intrigue us, and we will always need those who dream, and then go on to encounter the illusive, sometimes delusive, configurations of what we take to be real.

Angelo hauled his cab up to a halt in front of the Air Canada doors at the terminal.

"Will you see him again?" he asked.

"I hope so."

"If you do, tell him I remember him."

I smiled, and said I would. I made a mental note—remember this man, record what he said.

"You think he'll come back? Run again?"

"I doubt it."

"He'd win. Easily."

"Maybe. But he knows his time is finished. Could we bring him back like Sir John A for one last campaign? The old warrior. Well, there are different players now. Trudeau knew when to get out. Someone else has to come up with ideas for this country."

Angelo leaned over the seat, gazing back, while I climbed out to the curb.

"I tell you I worry. Things are not so good here. Yes, yes, not terrible. Sure, I make a living. Sure, I have a good life. Business is pretty good for me. But my children, their children, I worry. What will be here for them someday?"

I stopped, half in the cab, half out, and said truthfully I didn't know either, but I hoped for the best. I had children, and often wondered about what they would inherit.

Then I paid him, tipped him, thanked him, said goodbye, clambered out fully, entered the airport, joined the lineup for Toronto—a serpentine sprawl that looked like an urgent exodus—and mused on the mysteries of the soul, and the unexpected links we make with people, like Trudeau, who live public lives, realizing how difficult it is to truly grasp the essence of anyone, thinking that trying to resolve the mystery of a person is a wrong turn in thought, because the soul slips into the invisible, and compassion must come from knowing you can't hold on to anyone or anything, that we all pass one another, never quite knowing what it is we can or will make of ourselves or for ourselves, whether it is a destiny or a place in life, a family and a home, a business or a venture into the wilderness, the vocation to teach or the vocation to learn, a grand theory of the universe or a clear perception of a tree, a poem or a country.

*

We were to meet for lunch in the summer of 2000.

I'd cleared the time to travel to Montreal, though I'd hesitated for months to intrude on your grief. Michel had died towards the end of 1998. And I knew you had asked for time to mourn and heal. But in the late spring of 2000 I thought you might want to take a walk, and share time talking once more about books and ideas.

Mutual friends told me of your decline. They had described a grief so deep that it cut into your concentration and attention. You had become gentle, and distracted. I'd written a note indicating the dates when I would be free. From Ms. Sansoucy I received a friendly confirmation that the lunch was on. In spite of growing rumours about your ill health, I adjusted my plans accordingly, going on with my writing.

In July I wrote to you again to confirm the times. Two weeks later I received a short note. (Your letters always arrived in a distinctive, unpretentious envelope, with no insignia or symbolism. Sometimes there was simply a tiny red imprint with your name and address on it. Sometimes "pet" had been typed out over the letterhead address that said Heenan Blaikie.)

Dear Bruce,

Thank you for your letter of July 5 last. I am too busy with my sons in the summer to be able to give you a date. Let us wait until autumn.

All the best,
Pierre

Disappointed, I still understood the priority you attached to life with your children. It was a feeling we shared. You had once encouraged me to make my parenting commitments clear—to my children, and to myself. "Anyone can be Prime Minister, but only I could be the father to my children," you'd said, repeating almost word for word what you once said on TV. (What you said in public often wandered into what you said in private.) So I filed your note away, and made an entry in my records to call you in September. We could arrange for another time in the autumn.

But there was no more time.

On the twenty-eighth of September came the news of your passing.

Eulogy

September 30, 2000

He's gone. And we are rushing to judgment. We want to understand those years when he challenged and provoked us, when he bewildered and inspired us. We would like to comprehend his legacy, what the experience meant and means. Pierre Elliott Trudeau is gone, and we grapple now with memory. In this period of mourning, we also grapple with our future.

I've often thought over the past weeks about this day. What would I say about a friend who was our Prime Minister, a man who left office a long time ago? I've been asked, over and over, in the past days, to offer conclusions, evaluations, commentaries, contemplations. I can say he has been a part of my life since I was a boy. I first met him at the Liberal convention in Ottawa in 1968, when he was elected leader of the Liberal Party, and Prime Minister. In 1985, in Montreal, I met him again to talk over lunch about his years in politics. He invited me back, and after that we met and talked many times.

I can't say we were confidants, but I thought he was my friend and he certainly knew I was his. He sometimes offered advice, insights into ideas, politics, philosophy, the media. We talked at length about family and children, marriage and friendship, and of course about our country, which we thought rich with a promise beyond that of any other modern democratic state. Sometimes when I felt lost, or low, I'd phone him, and he'd promptly answer, and we'd talk, and though I seldom burdened him with my difficulties, he always graciously provided an intelligent, clear-eyed response. This was in its way a solace. Now that he has passed I must grapple with what he meant to me.

If I were a political historian, I might be able to provide a more informed overview of Trudeau. Perhaps I could assign the right ranking to his position among Canadian Prime Ministers. Perhaps I could tell you without equivocation what his policies and initiatives must mean for us. I could offer analyses that would satisfy academics and critics. But the truth is my sense of him remains deeply personal. What I write here is more of an elegy for one I took to be a courageous visionary. I've inklings of what his legacy might be, but I can only speak truly of what he stood for in my life.

When I was growing up in Canada through the late 1960s and the 1970s, and when I was young in the 1980s, he was our Prime Minister. His tenure was interrupted, of course. But primarily he was the one who was constant, there. At a very early age I had decided I wanted to write and teach—to live deliberately, and take on transcendental expeditions. Except that I was stumbling around, fumbling in an absurd dark. In those days people thought and talked a lot about authenticity and alternative lives. Trudeau had entered our scene like a surge of energy, and the times opened for us, and welcomed him. He insisted that we be proud of our true difference, and he proposed a politics of higher-self engagements and aspirations. There was an aura of theatre about him. He was conscious of the effect you could have through public symbolism. His pirouette behind the Queen, whether planned or unplanned (it doesn't matter), was a symbolically independent, republican gesture. Somehow his message was about igniting the spirit of our time and place.

Yes, he could be contradictory, and divisive. The human rights advocate was also the man who imposed the War Measures Act. The architect of centralized economic policies, like the National Energy Program (so vilified by the American oil corporations who had invested heavily in the western provinces), was also the cautious economic steward. He seemed to offer a promise for many that he never quite delivered.

Yet I can't say he disappointed me. When I was searching for a mythic model for myself—someone whose spirit I could absorb and transmute into my own—I turned more to him than to any Canadian author or artist. Frankly, for a young writer trying to find his breath and beat, I found there were few figures I could look to within our borders for guidance or elucidation, for maverick challenge or style and soulfulness.

The Americans had legions of angels and demons for a writer to emulate, or sidestep. Think of them: Emerson, Thoreau, Emily Dickinson, Whitman, Harriet Beecher Stowe, Hemingway, Thomas Wolfe, Gertrude Stein, T.S. Eliot, William Carlos Williams, Jack Kerouac; and in culture and politics there were the Kennedys, Martin Luther King Jr., Thomas Merton, Georgia O'Keeffe, Joan Baez,

Bob Dylan. No Canadian came close to them for me; none provided the spark I thought original and daring. Yes, at times, I looked to Marshall McLuhan, for apocalyptic brilliance; at times to Leonard Cohen, for his melding of mordant wit and soul ache; to Neil Young and Joni Mitchell, and the voices that summoned Kafka's Hunger Artist; to Irving Layton for his extravagant passions; and to the many Margarets. I kept hoping Saul Bellow would come back to Canada so that we could reclaim him.

But the one model of grace and self-discipline, of eloquence and commitment, of authenticity and intelligence, of solitary philosophical reflectiveness and public playfulness, of rage and vision, was Trudeau.

During our conversations I found him sharp and strong-minded, often combative and blunt. Once I made the mistake of suggesting that Prime Minister Brian Mulroney had something in common with Mackenzie King. Both were disliked by voters, yet voted back into power. Both were limited in their personalities and in their capacities for eloquence, but capable of forging coalitions, and of forcing through their agendas. Trudeau blinked, stared, straightened up in his chair, leaned back, and then launched into a twenty-minute defence of the progressive politics of King. His knowledge of King's initiatives and tactics was incisive and nuanced. I sat back, slightly stunned by the onslaught of prickly logic. It quickly dawned on me that Trudeau was defending himself.

He loved argument and dialogue. We would find ourselves discussing Henry Adams and Thomas Jefferson (who seemed to be particularly fascinating to him), then move on to movies—I remember him being struck by *The Mission* and *Saving Private Ryan*—and on again into literature and history. He liked to talk about the mystics St. Augustine and Teilhard de Chardin. And over and over we would share our enthusiasm for the potential of Canada.

It should be no surprise to know that politics was a rough game for him. On occasions, over our Chinese food lunch—it was always what we chose to eat, for reasons obscure to me—I would get glimpses of the effect of long service in the public realm: the disappointments, the sense of lost opportunities, the wonder over whether this cause or that policy did harm, the misunderstood communications, the bruising moments.

People speak of his emotional detachment. I felt this about him too. It was never a mean-spirited detachment, however. It came from his deep love for solitude. He respected this side in others. I love my solitude, and I thought that he grasped how important it is for people to know how to be alone, to find moments for rest and reverie, soul restoration. Once he retired, he really had left the political game. At times I thought him content.

After 1997 I began to find him frail. He was conscious of how people remembered him—those images of Trudeau sprinting away from the press and pressing crowds. This self-consciousness made him shy. I don't know what afflicted him, but whenever we met he was unfailingly cordial, and lucid. Rarely did I see him become hostile or rude, never ungrateful or cruel.

*

What would Trudeau himself say about retrospectives and eulogies? He wasn't much for dwelling on the past.

1998.

I visited him in Montreal, and told him of the Trudeau Era Conference about to be held at Toronto's York University. He looked at me skeptically. Then he said, in a mild chide,

"Don't you have something better to do with your time?"

He read over the conference's mission statement, which Professor David Shugarman (of York's Political Science Department) and I had composed. There were five principal points. The first three had to do with him, his legacy, and impact; the other two had to do with Canada and her political future.

He studied the statement for some time.

"Well, those last two points certainly interest me."

Those last two points didn't mention him at all.

This was Trudeau too, always facing the future. He let the energies of existence take him, and it was up to us to carry on, to find that spirit too, and the intelligence, goodwill, imagination and courage, to continue. Canada was a new proposition for him. It had a speculative destiny to thrive in a way different from, say, the United States, in a test that mixed the legacies of the English, French, aboriginals and those of other ethnic roots. To lose the hope and opportunity of our experiment, the measures of distinctiveness, was for him more tragic than any particular policy of his. At his best he did understand that he stood for more than his actual achievements in practical politics.

I must say here, forcefully, that I don't believe that Trudeau's vision of a Canada with a degree of political independence was accepted by the financial establishment, the corporate elites. During the hectic time when we organized the Trudeau conference at York, we tried to raise money from financial institutions. None would help directly. We ran a debt. It was the office of the vice-president of External at York that provided most of our money. Many prominent intellectuals and writers wouldn't come. They were reluctant to go on record about Trudeau. Some who did come spent a lot of time calling Trudeau an overrated failure. Scholarly gatherings should be contentious and controversial. Yet I was struck by the idea that Trudeau was a failure. By what standard a failure?

After the conference's first night, I returned to my office at Winters College. (The college had been named, ironically enough, for Robert Winters. He was the businessman who had run a vigorous second to Trudeau at the

Mystic Trudeau / 157

convention of 1968.) I talked briefly with the cleaning lady. She asked me how the event was going. I asked her what she thought of Trudeau. She said she had come to Canada, from Jamaica, in part because of him.

"My opinion of him? To the best of his ability," she said, "when you think of how corrupt politics can be, he tried to tell the truth. I respected that. I always tried to understand the arguments he made so I could make up my own mind."

(Though I almost said something about his penchant for antics and for his well-known distortions of biographical facts, I knew what she meant. In the political realm, during election fights, he didn't try to mislead.)

Her words were then, and are now, a fitting epitaph.

Was he difficult? Proud? Evasive? Even strange? Was he at times not up to the calling that drew him at once forward and inward? Yes, those flaws existed in him on an often grand scale.

And now when we struggle to find ways of saying goodbye, I'm sure the usual suspects will say he was an unfulfilled Prime Minister. The elites will assure us that the idea of Canada is irrelevant to the new global economic order. Followers of another political party tell us that we will strengthen ourselves by ignoring our history, our traditions, our mythologies, our culture and vision, and by following the American way. We are lectured by pundits in the media about the necessity of being realistic about economic globalism. The elites will tell us, "Don't worry. We are in control. We can't afford the kind of political leader that Trudeau embodied." Critics say he was just another politician, albeit a stylish one. He was part of the machine. Don't misplace your need for transcendence.

Yet where I live, in Stouffville, a small town in Ontario, and in the places where I talk and teach, and read and speak, the Trudeau myth persists. It not only persists, it grows. There is an abiding feeling in most people for one perceived to have the strain of eminence in him. We may disagree with him, even dislike him, but few doubt that when he was Prime Minister he spoke for Canada. In those times when I meet people, never once do I hear anyone anywhere say that they want to be anything other than Canadian. Who will speak for the idea of a country again?

*

Once during a CBC radio interview with Peter Gzowski, you were asked,

"How would you like to be remembered?"

You answered, quietly, and poignantly,

"I'd be happy if my children remember me."

Well, Pierre, many will remember you. They will recall the question Who speaks for Canada? I'll remember you for your courage and focus, for your spirited insistence that we should find a greatness of heart and mind. And I'll remember you for the generous time you spent talking to me. The controversies about you will continue. This is good, a sign of relevance. Through the squabbles and squalls, the rush and amplifications, the clowning and the fatigue, the delusions and illusions, the exaltations and degradations of the public life, you never let go of the idea that our higher selves could speak through us.

It may be that your vision of Canada won't endure—who said one vision should be permanent?—but it was an attempt to say, We are here: this is the promise and price of our bold process. You carried that message forward with considerable conviction and will, with often contradictory and perplexing actions, in sometimes allusive phrases and acutely intelligent arguments.

*

And for us—after? We take Canada too much for granted. Perhaps our future will bring on the fight for another kind of openness in the millennium. Our imaginations must enlarge too, so that we may recognize that some of what we were attracted to in Trudeau is what we are ourselves: subtly rebellious, inward, sometimes anarchic, people who chafe at definitions and prohibitions, spiritual solitaries who nevertheless seek links, privileged people who surely want to move beyond colonized mentalities and timidity. Perhaps the constitutional imperative of the Charter must lead to republicanism, the next stage in our cultural and social maturity. Trudeau said we had much to show and share with others: our spirit must not be thwarted by tribal animosities or provincial self-absorption.

When I heard of his passing, I mourned my friend. "*Cast a cold eye/On life, on death,/Horseman, pass by,*" Yeats wrote in "Under Ben Bulben," a poem that was one of Trudeau's most beloved. Death, pass us by, pass on, the poet meant, but permit some part of our spirit and actions to remain. I hope we will remember the questions Trudeau asked. The way we answer will change and move us. And we should remember that, yes, we are on our own now, but not entirely: a vivid memory is part of his legacy.

We Are the Images

It began in images, and it ended in symbolism.

It began in impressions, fleeting but quickening, and ended in iconography and analogy, heart-centres in the cosmos of strands and correspondences. Make your method one based on analogy, and you will always be compelled to rethink and reconstruct. "Appearances are a glimpse of what is hidden" (Anaxagoras).

While I continue to deal with the implications of Trudeau's legacy, I engage the images we have of him and made of him. There were so many. From 1968 on we were overwhelmed by pictures, poses, feeds, stills, scenes, cover stories, film clips, iconic outlines and profiles.

How does a person become mythic? Other leaders have dominated their times and places. But why does one figure become endowed with so much force, engaging our projections? How does a person go from human to living in the sensational intersections of mythic reference? Why do some people get lifted above the daily tread of activities? Their lives—people who walk around and breathe the same air that we do—become magnified. The public story begins to take on metaphysical shape.

Why certain people take on this allure is confounding. It's as if these figures directly attract the energies of the Universal Spirit. At one time we would have called such a figure a shaman, or an elder. Stir into this alchemical mix the amplifying powers of the e-media, and its cascades and volume of pictures and sound, and it will feel as if the spirit is kicking into us, while we flail and wrestle with the trails of its mystique.

*

"I cannot now think symbols less than the greatest of all powers whether they are used consciously by the masters of magic, or half-consciously by their successors . . ." (Yeats). Let us say that the e-media is now the agency of magic, and that its masters and users are half-conscious of its workings and effects.

We witnessed Trudeau's transformations through the media, both electronic and print. Powerful and influential, the e-flow, in fluid arrays of faces and postures, events and memorials, can inspire sudden emotions. Certain images achieve reverberant conditions. The presence of a person (existence on the horizontal plane of society, politics, work, judgments, personal relations) can meet with the vertical plane (the soul-dimension, the domains of myth, poetry, what we may say is the sacred); and in those critical junctures, our minds resound with associations and echoes. It is then that we say that experience has depth. We become aware, often abruptly, that we are engaging something more than an image. We have crossed over into symbolism. The Greek word *Symbolon* means the halves of a broken piece of pottery. One part of the physical object rests in the physical world, the other part in the invisible. Symbolic moments are those events when we are conscious that life has taken on powerful metaphoric vibrations. Life feels heightened. We sense that we are being struck open, in our hearts, or drawn upwards, away from the cracked world. Every meeting of the vertical and horizontal planes is a layering of realms, in the ritual crux. These are the experiences that seem to move us beyond matter, into a spiritual stream.

What images and symbols did Trudeau spark in our imaginations? What rituals did we experience through the dramas of his life in the energy fields of electricity?

Here is James Hillman, inspired and eloquent in his book *Emotion*, on the matrix moment, when we watch images moving on a screen, and emotions like visitations descend upon us,

> Events are not mere energetic facts without aim; they are emotional intensities with intention. If energy is the one universal reality present everywhere, then emotion is too . . . The symbol is not something "outside" which arouses emotion "inside." Outside in the world, emotions are apprehended as symbolic qualities; inside in the person, symbols are lived out in emotions . . . the realm of emotion cannot be limited to the "within" . . . This is a moment of truth, a moment of transcendence in which inner and outer, conscious and unconscious, are linked by symbol and lived as conscious emotion.

Movements in ourselves like chemical reactions, susceptibility, attraction, repulsion: each person in his or her viewing room can become inextricably linked to processes (ecstasies, crises) occurring far away. People call the magical effects of images and energies occult because their effects on us are intangible. Yet we feel the burn. We live impressed.

Can we penetrate the batteries of images, the hieroglyphs of our speeding space-time?

Let me propose guidance for media magic and hieroglyphics: the fourfold awareness that Dante expounded in *Epistola X*, to the poet Can Grande, in the *Convivio*. This is the decoding process proposed by McLuhan in the last chapter, "Media Poetics," of *Laws of Media*. It is the method also retrieved by Frye, in the last chapter of *The Great Code*, titled with his typical understatement, "The Order of Types: Language II."

Images can operate on a literal, transient level. They can be immediate, visceral, their glamour and glitz becoming easily disposable, passing through the mind, leaving little trace. But images also possess a moral dimension, a lesson on how we are to live. The didactic dimension portrays the consequences of choices, lives spinning in their ethical tumble. This is the level of politics, and most sermons.

Allegory tells us that another story exists under the obvious tale. Images import allegorical subtexts, nuanced and referenced sub-stories, usually taken, in western traditions, from the Homeric myths, and the Ovidian metamorphoses, from Virgil's daring enlargements of Homer, and the Bible.

More profoundly there is the symbolic level. This is

drawn from deep wells of analogy and yearning. The symbolic is the most elusive of levels, the dimension of infinite linkage, where the mind is transported into "the forest of correspondences." In this metaphoric phrase, Baudelaire summons the tree of the Kabbalah, the intricate maze of being. Here emotion comes powerfully into us, because symbols operate on both mind and the senses, along the arteries of feeling, in transcendental reverberations. We engage the symbolic, and feel something greater at play. But because symbols point to the invisible, the experience feels uprooted, not continuous with what came before.

Thus we may whirl up from the mundane to the mystical, and back again. We may think of the upward and downward motion in terms of ascending or descending a staircase, or a ladder, Frye said. We may say it is like climbing a twisting rope, or following a thread. At the ends of these, at the edges . . . the invisible, the intangible . . . where you find you're in the break (or gulf) . . . where the metaphysical and the physical . . . may rub or slam together . . . Thus the world could become (perhaps; it's my hope) more than a universe of random, empty data, and recharge and transform into *sacra pagina*, where our lives once more become open to signals and signs.

The e-cosmos experience accelerates the intensity of intersecting planes at a matchless tempo. McLuhan understood how electronic processing restores the interpenetrations of the symbolic with the material plane. "My method is vertical rather than horizontal, so the scenery does not change but the texture does," he said.

The speed of moving images can be skin-tingling. It will jolt us into a caffeined-like nervousness, and it will numb us down into a mesmerized acceptance of anything. We live aphoristically, information compressed and moving at greater speeds. Images have the power to snare us. But images can act like seeds, becoming symbols, unfolding and blossoming later, providing that there is nurturing attention, the warmth of contemplation.

This hieroglyphic nature of images can be confusing for observers. The cruxes of the literal plane (the horizon of physical experience) and the symbolic plane (the whirlwind of possible meanings) defy the nihilism of consumerism, the parodic self-references of pop culture, academic deconstructions which attempt to keep interpretation only on the social and political level, and the homilies of preachers who (at all costs) want to preserve their definition of community.

Yet "the soul never thinks without a mental picture" (Aristotle). Our imaginations piece together the spin of bits, of images.

*

From the beginning we projected impressions onto Trudeau. We constantly made something of him. This process can't be automatically created. Recall the attempts by media handlers to turn Senator John Kerry into an icon during the American federal election of 2004. People were often curious and hopeful about Kerry, in his race against President George W. Bush. Neither deification nor demonization took hold. People could make nothing of him.

With Trudeau, voyeurism and the predatory camera, nervous mythifications and collective longings, combined to make someone larger than life. But like all whose lives take on mythic dimensions, he paid the price—his solitude invaded by the sorrows of family tragedy.

Trudeau said to me, "The style is the man." We are so accustomed to thinking that dealing with images and symbols is vulgar and frivolous, or trivializing, a counterfeit violation of the supremacy of the word, that we forget how meaning is not only verbal or linguistic. Wilde's Lord Henry has a witty reply to such reductions in *The Picture of Dorian Gray*: "It is only shallow people who do not judge by appearances. The true mystery of the world is the visible, not the invisible." The word "appearance" links with "apparition." It in turn links with the Greek word for image, *eidolon*. This refers to the substitute, what stands in for the invisible realm. Wilde's praise of surfaces is placed in the mouth of amoral Lord Henry. We shouldn't confuse the character with the author. Wilde was, nevertheless, uncanny in his ability to anticipate the epic simulations and exhibitionist fantasies that we ingest. In *The Picture of Dorian Gray*, the portrait of Dorian, while hidden in an attic, stalks the mind of its errant subject. In the finale to the novella, the image appears to murder him. Wilde (atypically) makes no authorial comment at the end of the story, leaving us to contemplate the Mystery powers of symbols and apparitions.

To become fascinated suggests attachment—to fasten ourselves to what glows and mystifies, and yet beckons and compels. In Trudeau's case our fascination was with transformation.

He was the most private of leaders who led the most public of existences. He became part of the subterranean and obvious changes in Canada, a country expanding into consciousness of its potential and originality.

Other Prime Ministers have had their imagistic effects on our imagination. Stephen Harper ("Steve" to his good buddy G.W. Bush) immediately became the bland leader. Earthbound, stolid, his deliberate dullness concealed hard intelligence. "The zero charisma man" was how his spin doctors promoted him.

Paul Martin had the right initials: "PM." When he found (rare) moments of calm in public, he had an avuncular senior's style. Ominously, his initials conjured an imminent "Post Mortem." Martin's mythic projections were erratic. His jumpiness kept interfering with our focus.

Jean Chrétien's image was that of the unbreakable Machiavel. He skirted the ethical lines between guile and vindictive calculation. While remarkably successful in his machinations over three elections and many years in power, Chrétien's image had the limited resonance of the "Iron Man."

Brian Mulroney, with his free trade initiative—a profound change in the country's consciousness—was the slick operator. The suave corporatist, his image oozed charm and oiled its way out the door (of perception). It sometimes seemed that people wanted to scrub Mulroney clean from all mythic projection.

Trudeau's face lent itself well to caricature. When we first encountered him, on the federal political scene in 1967 and 1968, while he was Justice Minister in Pearson's cabinet, and then when he became the callow PM, we were apt to be engaged by his wit and fast-car insolence. Images branded these impressions liberal, free and individual. We were skeptical enough to know some of the facts: he was part political novice and part scholar, in part a product of that split English and French background, embodying the divisions of a society and culture polarized along linguistic lines. Enemies called him "lazy, spoiled, and subversive" (Maurice Duplessis). Initially he was a 1960s hipster—vaguely romantic, hypersexual. But there were tinges of severity in his handlings of legal reforms and separatists. In his first years in power, when the War Measures Act was imposed in 1970 (at the request of Quebec Premier Robert Bourassa), the seeming imp became the combatant. He had slipped from representing unfettered liberty to hierarchy and the representation of the power of the state to protect everyone. This transformation was a sharp turn. Thereafter the defiant youthful images of Trudeau would be shadowed by images of his defence of order. In those impressions he became the guardian—dangerous, solid. He was the elder who wouldn't hesitate to draw the line, and who had (apparently) masked himself behind a maverick's sheen. The attack on the terrorist cell the FLQ was successful. They never emerged again. This was his symbolic rupture with revolutionary ideologues who had thought that he might be one of theirs.

In those turbulent years Trudeau showed Janus-like capabilities. He had a radical doubleness in his persona that ensured mythic survival. Brian Mulroney, Jean Chrétien, Paul Martin and Stephen Harper shared an inability to transform themselves through their images. They remained largely what they had been when they began. Their images deepened into archetypes, but never fundamentally altered: Mulroney would remain the slick mechanic, the facilitator of deals; Chrétien would always be the wily schemer, whose fractured English mirrored the increasingly multilingual population; Martin was the business tycoon addled by too much concern, for whom everything beyond boardroom economics was a surprise;

Harper was so anti-charismatic—the cold man of political realism—that any change in his appearance was considered odd. These archetypes were rooted in material concerns. But individuals of heightened sensitivities, whose energies appeal to many people simultaneously, often must bear the charge and weight of spiritual transference. People add more to the story, sketching in more links, building bridges for the ambiguities and the gaps in information, amplifying and embroidering.

Trudeau turned his public life into a personal rite of passage. When he was twenty-nine he journeyed to the East, learning yoga and meditation techniques; these he practised for the rest of his life. And when he entered politics he became a show-off, mugging and flirting with pretty women in front of cameras. He was the colourful dandy who was a tough election campaigner (he fought the 1980 federal election without bothering to appear in many commercials, and without agreeing to debate then Prime Minister Joe Clark). He was the constitutional proponent of individual rights who could become an autocrat.

He spoke of reason—the calling of the higher intelligence—and then willingly played off the wild emotions of crowds. Here was a man with a passionate temper (given to lashing out at others physically) who became a world-peace advocate. He was the self-contained bachelor who eventually married a much younger woman. Through the highly publicized divorce he became the suffering father, the single parent who left meetings early to be with his three sons. He had craved liberty when he was a young man, refusing to be tied down to anyone or anything, and he married a young gypsy, who would one day insist on those liberties for herself. The man who became leader because he understood the power of images found his ex-wife, Margaret, would strike back at him through images. She became a photographer and an actress in films. She posed on the front of fashion magazines, and was sometimes photographed at clubs in luridly exposed situations. We intuitively responded to Trudeau's dualities, calling them complexity, recognizing that they were another source of charisma, and of endless speculation.

The mystic and the dandy are closely allied. Both travel camouflaged; both intimate that more is going on than meets the eye. They are often conflicted by social custom and the command of inwardness; they follow courses that seem contradictory to others. A mystic is a contrarian, and must be; "gone, gone," the other shore compels him. The dandy will dress up, behaving outrageously to defy expectations. One becomes contrary through the metaphysical imperative; the other, through the charm of style. It is rare to find such strains in one person, but Trudeau had them, and so he emerged into our attention tattooed with strangeness.

The visionary and the solitary are linked. In the privacy of the mind a person may dream, but the public actor must submit to existential scripts, fact and compromise. Walk away from roots, from your social conditioning, and you may feel impelled to keep moving, away, and on. . . . To what? The inward space no fact may disturb, the unlimited dream. Thus the visionary will prize privacy, long ambles in the snow, walks down streets or along forest trails, treks in the wilderness, time alone with a book or a notebook.

When does solitude become merely loneliness? At a point no one else can ascertain. A mystic's solitude is populated. A lonely night is bare and hushed, fragile and desolating.

*

When I first began to have lunch with Trudeau in 1985, he had exiled himself from public scrutiny, so he thought. The Liberal Party, defeated in the last federal election (1984), was in disarray under John Turner. Prime Minister Mulroney's neo-conservative policies were ascendant. Outside of power, Trudeau nevertheless exerted a magnetic influence from the sidelines. He was much more protective of his political legacy than he liked to let on. Our conversations reminded me of how his mythic powers could be verbal: he had the lawyer's love of courtroom rhetoric and the vehemence of the natural polemicist. Nevertheless, it was his image (his theatrical appearances at social gatherings on the arms of beautiful young women) and his symbolic interventions (coming out of retirement to dispute the Meech Lake and Charlottetown Accords, both of which had put to the test his vision of the Charter, and thus of Canada herself) that often superseded his verbal skills. Paramount was his ability to make his presence felt. The less he said, the greater the mystique. The more he withdrew, the greater the speculations. The more focused his occasional polemics became, the more ferocious his mind seemed. When he intervened in debates on the nature of the Constitution, he did offer reasoned arguments, albeit punctuated with contempt. But what people remember was the fire in the presentations of his image. One magazine cover (*Maclean's*, September 1992) showed him staring back—that paternal daimon. His enraged eyes asked us to choose, what kind of country do you want to have? What route will you follow? Conscience works best when it is silent, compelling us to look inward. Turning inward, we engage the imagination, the mediator between calling and action. The image of Trudeau staring us down arguably did more to unsettle the Mulroney initiatives in constitutional revision than did all the editorials written at the time.

*

He wanted privacy for the finale of his drama. Perhaps he understood that few people withstand the hunting eyes and eavesdropping ears of the insatiable, omnipresent media. (Yet another point I didn't know how to raise when I visited him.) E-communications baptize, penetrate, swallow, cruelly consume. The interstices of the vertical and the horizontal can be traumatic to some—the intensity overpowering. Even he, in spite of his evasiveness and his self-discipline, couldn't entirely withdraw inside the boundaries of an ordinary existence, his careful removal into retirement. His son's drowning was a mythic passing in itself; the father's risk-taking had been passed on to a son who would be dragged down into the waters by the weight of his backpack. The public, sensitive to Trudeau's transformations from youthful voyager and daredevil to a statesman mauled by loss, obsessively followed his son's funeral as if in a premonition of the passing of "the father of the new national identity" (Monique and Max Nemni).

Media images infuse us with ritual processes, ceremonial passages. Meanings converge. We are unprepared for the 24–7–365 Mystery initiations. And yet we are instilled with their descents, their auras of destiny, their energies and elevations, their synchronicities, their portents that appear like benedictions or warnings, the constellations in the cosmos of mind and emotion.

The circulation of images and symbols is the primary currency of the global amphitheatre, replacing money.

The media Mysteries amplified the vertical dimension in Trudeau's life. His demands for eminence and excellence had sometimes compelled people to look beyond themselves. When he died almost two years after his son's passing, we perpetuated the rite of farewell, reverberations that came from a shared knowledge of sorrow. His funeral in Montreal, and the oration at the ceremony by his son Justin, confirmed what many people had felt had been stirring since news of his illness. We were also mourning a portion of our dreams and our projections.

A life of depth and intensity must carry a cost.

In return for his commitment to a dramatic existence, we bestowed on Trudeau's story the vestige and tone of transcendence. This process frustrates political scientists and historians who look at government policy and social and psychological motives alone. Our images of him, for better or worse (rather, for better and worse), through the contrary energies he embodied, and through the reforging glare of the media, had become symbols. He had moved, and we had moved with him, from snapshot glimpses of enthusiasm—when he was a candidate running, taunting, throwing out ideas, dispensing contempt, challenging custom, summoning the powers, electronic and elemental—to the symbol of a flawed leader sunk into melancholy over his inability to save his son. Trudeau's strangeness had come in part from his changeability, his iconic appearance, his availability to our projections, his inward calling which we implicitly recognized, all the pitches of life caught in its contradictions.

Every citizen viewer with a reanimating imagination had guessed, or perceived, that the processing of mystery had engulfed us.

*

Pierre, a good portion of anyone's life is lived inward. The *Upanishads* talk of "turning the globes of the eyes back to front." This is so we may look inside but also turn to recognize what is there. What is there? . . . a sensory paradise, and jumble. How easy it is to drown in chatter, to be swept up by routine, or ritual.

In your understanding of Teilhard de Chardin, and in your study of Mounier's Personalism, you recognized that we had arrived at a summit in time. The summit is also an abyss. The boundaries between private mind and global consciousness are disappearing. The mystic secrets are being exposed: emptiness and fullness, vibration and reception, energy and depletion, the intensities of light and darkness. In this process each of us became one and many. A part of us would be alone and a part of us would be other. Viewing spaces would be crowded by spirits and reflections. Our own communication devices admitted the unbounded energy of the beyond.

You lived one part in the whirlwind of images, one part in the orderly concern of your familiar solitude. But the line between the two realms kept breaking down. Can anyone fully learn to endure this yoking together of dimensions, of realms, of sides, of worlds?

To look deeply inside a person is nearly impossible. This is part of ineffable experience too. If we are so unknowable, then what can we say of those energies that rove into us and sometimes harrow? So we resort again to metaphors and symbols.

We are souls in dialogue, with two forms of consciousness perpetually operating—the observer and the participant.

Pierre, we were piercing observers of your life, and painfully became participants in your epiphanies and rituals.

*

The soul hungers for images.

The overflowing images and symbols of the e-cosmos intimate the oceanic—the boundlessness that shatters attempts at static frames of reference.

We are not only asking the identity question of ourselves, but of what we are receiving from what is, possibly, beyond the human.

Images and symbols form the language of mythology. Through electricity in the e-cosmos, pervasive communications meld into intuited communions. There are messages whose codes seem sometimes to be without a key, streaming away from our grasp. Yet through these apparently haphazard infusions, we apprehend the mystery thrall. It is this pulse that moves us ever deeper into those interpenetrating moments where intimations of new mythologies begin.

Trudeau's life had been translated from personal history into the impersonal shape of universal drama. He was determined to achieve greatness (his notebooks confirm) and equally determined to preserve his solitude. He lived in the intersections of myth and crisis in a way few wish to, and ever do. The result was the paradox of being at once intimate with his life's dramatic turns and distant from his soul's route.

And will we be able to say one day that these images and symbols helped to shape a country?
 And will they remind us in years to come that we have one?

North of the Future

The cortege edged out slowly.
 On the October morning, VIA train 638 departed from the Ottawa terminal. It left behind a small group of mourners, and gathered speed, to make its way through

fields and towns to Notre-Dame Basilica in Montreal.

Soon the cortege had to slow again so that mourners, who had assembled along the tracks, could watch the train that carried Trudeau's coffin.

In hayfields, near factories, at level crossings, by crossroads, on platforms, on the roofs of cars and on the back of pickup trucks, people gathered. Some stood alone with small flags or a small sign in hand. I had the impression, while I watched this on TV, that many people were pulling back, seeking a space away from the curious who had come together in crowds. A vigil was being kept. One hand-scrawled sign, caught in an instant, said, "Going home."

Even in death he surprised us. His pilgrimage was still in our eyes and minds.

People felt an absence. Some part of their time and place had gone missing, being translated elsewhere.

Beside the railroad tracks people called out to the train, and to his sons, Justin and Alexandre, who were in the rail car, among friends and family members.

The fire and the rose passed by.

*

Yet people couldn't forget his pillaging zeal in winning at almost any cost. This wasn't the passing of a saint, a poet, a philosopher, a hockey star, a humble sage. A leader had died, one known for his pride, and for his belief in what he called a just society.

What were we lamenting that day? Why did people say that they felt afterwards as if they were without a guide? Were we mourning a man, who had, after all, both alienated and galvanized others? Were we honouring a country that we knew could be more?

By the railway tracks, through fluid TV and Internet images, through the static photographs of newspapers and magazines, in the grist of commentators' voices, in the fleeting talk in the streets, people often thought they were saying goodbye to one person's dream, a premise of a country. The tele-acoustic media, in the spectacle of its ahistorical now, had scorched us with grieving. We saw the lifting of the coffin by solemn RCMP guards, the red rose draped on the red and white flag, the son's weeping, the silent daughter following behind the casket. Later in press commentaries and interviews we heard the acknowledgment by foes that Trudeau's beliefs angered them enough to become sharper in their counter-arguments.

Images and symbols are forms of knowledge, so I've been exploring. This is *gnosis*, direct seeking and knowing, where personal experience is heightened to transforming consciousness of patterns. But the knowing is often intuitional. *Gnosis* is a heart-mystery, a spell we know even if we can't entirely explain it.

"*Those masterful images because complete/Grew in pure mind, but out of what began?*" Yeats asks in "The Circus

Animals' Desertion." He answers his own question: they rise unexpectedly from "a mound of refuse or the sweepings of a street . . . old bottles, and a broken can . . ." Certain images, however, rise into consciousness more profoundly than others. They ascend into the mind's eye from where "all the ladders start . . . in the foul rag-and-bone shop of the heart." This is the poet's apogee image for the interpenetrations of vertical and horizontal information. "Old bones, old rags," the sweepings of the street, are informed then lifted by the heart. The ladder could be a staircase, a tower, a spiral net, a tree, a cord, an antenna. We trace these metaphorically to reach other states of mind, and then descend back to the physical realm. Yeats is invoking the power poetic images have to tear reality apart, and to remake it according to the currents of the invisible.

When images become symbols they become energy-centres of ideas and emotions. Consultants and producers sell celebrity glitz, transmitting it via TV or Internet, in advertising flyers or on billboards, so that images float unanchored, seemingly haphazard. Yet for an image to become iconic, no longer a mere sense impression—for it to become a representation of depth—it must enter into the intricate matrix of projection and identification, memory and desire. It has to possess tracks of the past; it has to catch the elusive present, and carry some prophetic inklings of the shape of things to come.

When VIA train 638 left Ottawa for Montreal, we

were drenched in the colours of autumn mourning, red and gold. We had identified Trudeau with the fire of mind (represented by the rose he wore in his lapel), and with metamorphosis (his adeptness at transforming himself). These merged into what was for many an outpouring of anxious hope about Canada itself. How could our experiment survive in the new world economic order? He had changed yet again, temporarily, into a martyr for the unease we felt about our country's future.

In a few short weeks after the funeral, a federal election was called by Prime Minister Chrétien. The cortege led us into a time of introspection, "the soul in paraphrase, the heart in pilgrimage" (George Herbert). The lexical links in "mourning" lead to Anglo-Saxon roots, to care, grieve, and other roots, to remember, to long for. Mourning, like ecstasy, like suffering, is another mood that can enlarge us. In thoughtful lament experience widens. But an election swiftly brings people down to earth, as it were.

Chrétien wanted to hold the election in the autumn of 2000 "to confirm a legacy and to affirm Canadian values." During the fall campaign, the leaders of the political parties went on to define voters in consumerist terms. We were marketplace beings, no longer citizens, but clients, or customers, out shopping for a better style of noninvasive government. Liberty had come to mean the right to spend money in whatever way we saw fit. In the hype and hyperbole, there was no debate about the good, about an opened country, no pictures painted of what government must do, no questions raised about justice or emergent personality.

While I pondered the crests and depths of election images, I wondered, what were we being asked to give back? Where was the call beyond the pronouncements and innuendoes, the attack ads and photo ops?

*

Trudeau came to power to forge a new generational wager. His sense of vocation made him question structures that would not yield to change. "I shall make Statesmanship my profession and, if God permit, I shall know my profession well," he announced (to himself?) in a diary entry of 1945, while he was at Harvard. He made the powerful proposition to us: Could this country transcend ethnic rivalries and linguistic barriers? Could we enlarge the imaginative range of our geography, and our age?

When VIA train 638 rolled through the fall countryside, pundits didn't doubt the verity of the grieving and the vigils of those who stood along the tracks, in the fields. Yet pundits also said that a higher calling for ourselves, for a country, was likely irrelevant to financial self-concern. In the election campaign of that year, we heard much about economic policy. While this was surely important, one could not see how such proposals could form the basis of another generational wager, the gamble we sometimes take on our culture and time, when we feel the urgings to reach for more life, for more imagination, for more liberty, for more chances for our identities to flourish (or founder).

Conceive of what Canada had become by then. There was unparalleled prosperity, though unevenly distributed. Unprecedented government surpluses should have allowed us to probe values and directions. We had a Charter of Rights and Freedoms that contrasted dramatically with the Constitution of the United States. Our civility had largely permitted us to absorb the forces of the planetized economy and culture. Surpluses suggest abundance, and an abundance of wealth should serve and permit greater openness. We had mourned a man who had once asked us to think for ourselves, and to reach beyond ourselves. Where could vision lead? What images would recur to disquiet us?

*

"Just watch me," Trudeau snapped to a reporter in 1970, on the steps of Parliament, when he was asked how far he would go with the War Measures Act.

We absorb images then store them for future retrieval. But one image may abide, like a persistent hallucination, becoming an indispensable part of our commentary, and our subconscious dreaming.

Let us gaze at one. And through gazing free an image from its archival status.

In May 1977, at a reception at Buckingham Palace, Trudeau pirouetted behind the back of a retreating Queen Elizabeth II.

This was a rude gesture to many. He had rehearsed his spin (according to Jim Coutts, his principal secretary from 1974 until 1981). Trudeau made it look spontaneous; and in a way it did look like the afterthought of an eternal schoolboy thumbing his nose at authority. The pirouette could have been a reinforcement of an inflated sense of self-importance. It was his ego refusing to submit to anything others defined. Still we should reflect on what depths of courage it must have taken to whirl away in the moment, when he knew that the photographers and their quick-response cameras were close, in a royalist hall of mirrors.

Consider this: the moment was an act of defiance that spoke in the code of ritual rebellion. It showed the fire in him, the unfolding rose of identity breaking through. The pirouette singled him out from other heads of government in attendance.

Imagine the questions embodied in this image of the turning away. For whom do leaders truly speak? To what ruling crowds do politicians belong?

Consider more: the Canadian Prime Minister spun away from the Queen, Prince Charles, Prince Philip (caught in the image glancing back, slightly aghast), and the Queen's attendants, in a gesture that showed resistance to embalmed ceremony and stiffened protocol. What ceremonies still carry the power to summon the invisible?

The image danced across the globe almost instantaneously. It affirmed contrariness, in an allegory of peaceful opposition. Turn the other way, uproot yourselves . . . It was a gesture that kept alive the idea of Canadians making their own destiny, reminding others—and ourselves—that we are capable of sheering away from established tracks.

What can an image transmitted across boundaries achieve? What elaborations through editorials and commentaries? The pirouette, Trudeau knew, would be an event and an issue, inflaming words.

Consider even more: his counter-spin image is another part of his legacy and part of our experience of metamorphic Canada. This should be the place, and the time, that in its turning away from others' forms and structures, re-creates patterns and paths in which we may counter stifling convention.

When Trudeau pivoted away behind the Queen, he made a pivotal gesture in the direction of Canada. He whirled to the west, and thus home.

Let us expand this gaze into the analogical powers of the image.

Consider a pictorial moment that had the opposite effect. When Prime Minister Brian Mulroney sang "When Irish Eyes are Smiling" with President Ronald Reagan on St. Patrick's Day at the Shamrock Summit in Quebec City (March 18, 1985), we saw images of the two leaders holding hands with their wives, and facing south. Mulroney turned to the United States. He smiled delightedly, and sang to the cameras. He looked towards the empire.

In this gesture he signalled deals and acceptance. Mulroney's moves were more than political realism, they seemed to be suggesting merger. The image said we must be entirely pragmatic: here's the dominant power of the western world, so let's go along with it.

The picture revealed, in implications that only multi-dimensional images may bring, a leader toadying, submitting his will to another's. Viewers felt a sense of betrayal. People said "their backs went up." The effect of the image was immediately sensational, and grating. I submit that Mulroney's image that night became a symbol of appeasement. His reputation never recovered from the searing instant.

In 1999, one hundred and forty-eight editors and broadcasters gave Trudeau the award Newsmaker of the Century in Canada. It was the image of the audacious turning away that helped him win that accolade.

Here is how he responded to the honour he must have known already belonged to him,

"I am at once surprised and quite pleased with the information."

Observe that he said "information" instead of "award." His response was flat, almost dismissive. This implies that the news was simply one more bit of data in the influx of imagery and stimulations that configure our new mythological array.

His pirouette away from royalist decorum (custom and expectation) was a seeding image. Once the mind is implanted with such an impression and idea, there is no arresting the process of how they may dwindle and disappear, to be eventually forgotten, or how they will prosper and leap from their origins, becoming irreversible in their gestations. The energy released may be greater than the seed.

The image of Trudeau's spin away from the Queen has been waiting for its reception and its re-creation.

*

Bishop Berkeley said, in his rejoinder to the scientific materialism (and the literalism) of his time, "We Irish think otherwise." Let us rewrite and update this to read, "We Canadians think otherwise." Institutions and laws should evolve along with the unfolding conditions of our intelligence, and the honing of our perceptions and awareness. I propose that a provocative point for us in the millennium could be the idea of establishing a republic in Canada. We could conceive of how we could mature politically, socially, culturally, and above all psychically, by throwing off royalty, the last vestige of colonization and empire.

Such a turning away would provide us with a generational wager. It could become our new deal, when we begin to look to ourselves for leadership and sustenance. Since military and economic independence are no longer options to us, then we must look to symbolism and cultural expression, to appeals to the imagination and extensions of our native stories. To fulfill the promise of our newness (a relative newness; we are an old democracy, with a spirit that emerges from coinciding civilizations, French, English, aboriginal and ethnic), we could imagine ourselves free enough to choose from our own, on our own.

If we moved to establish a republic, and divested ourselves of the trappings of royalty (call it offshore parenting), then I believe that the separatist cause in Quebec would quickly end. The separatists have for too long insisted that they have a monopoly on passion and vision, that appeal to distinctiveness and originality. In our Charter we find values—pluralism, minority rights. Add to these a longing for a strain of independence, and for our blend of stable democratic institutions and gradual non-violent transformation.

The question is can it be done?

On September 26, 2001, in his regular column for the *Globe and Mail*, the redoubtable Jeffrey Simpson said that independent act would be impossible. Our Constitution is highly, and necessarily, restrictive. Any changes to it would require the unanimous consent of the provincial premiers. Section 41, paragraph A, of the 1982 Constitution entrenched monarchy. The likelihood of notoriously disagreeable premiers consenting to anything was probably Utopian. "We are stuck with monarchy," Trudeau himself said, stoically.

He was ambivalent about monarchy. He said in 1971, in a CBC-TV interview, "I myself believe that the simplest and best solution now for Canada is to preserve the monarchy—we would be replacing it by what? . . ." He did go on to say, in that interview, that "one can't predict the future . . ." Yet he would also say, in 1971, "the world must be our constituency." Then earlier, in 1970, he would ask, "Is there some mysterious force in our character which drives us relentlessly in this introspective quest for our identity?" And there is the image of the pirouette.

But something had changed because of the Charter, perhaps unknown to the usually well-informed Simpson. The Secession Reference in the Supreme Court Judgment of 1998 set out the legal framework for separation. That framework showed that the process of constitutional reform could be achieved through referenda. It's probable that referenda on all issues would be unhealthy for our democracy, paralyzing its process by constant reviews of law and policy. Moreover, referenda on social issues (abortion, capital punishment) would be needlessly polarizing, and probably a violation of the Charter's guarantee of individual rights. Excessive dependence on referenda would also incite those end-of-the-world scenarios so beloved by insecure politicians anxious to demonstrate "iron and piety," in Robert Lowell's evocative description of the troubles that beset his America. On select initiatives, however, the referendum process could be an invaluable instrument.

A door had opened. The system had shifted. The Supreme Court declared that there is a requirement on the part of politicians to negotiate change if there is a referendum, with a clear question and a majority vote. In short, political consensus no longer has to be controlled, or even shaped, by politicians who refuse to consider certain issues of governance. In this judgment the Supreme Court judges themselves followed the suggestive outlines of the Charter that Trudeau planted in the Constitution Act of 1982.

Here is Trudeau in his 1990 essay, "The Values of a Just Society,"

> . . . And then we have a real country—that is, the unorganized coalition of Canadian individuals and groups scattered across the nation, for whom Canada is more than a collection of provinces . . .

Empower each person, and laws and institutions can be challenged, beyond the powers and set relations of federal politicians and jurisdictions.

*

1998.
Montreal.

"What are the premiers interested in?" Trudeau mused, when we talked about the divisions of power.

He didn't wait for me to reply.

"Their own power," he said.

Then in what seemed almost like an afterthought,

"People should be willing to go beyond the powers that be."

Even if the initiative were to be finally defeated in a referendum, the questioning of authority and structure through conferences and forums would inspire people to be engaged with the imaginative turn of their country.

Here's an oddity: the clause in the Constitution that mentions monarchy swears allegiance to the Queen, but not to her heirs. The British North America Act mentioned successors. Our Constitution doesn't. What was subtly left available? Did Trudeau know that one day we would find the gap that could represent a potential break from the past?

Kindle this notion: What would it mean to affirm our eccentric solitudes through an exchange on the premises of republicanism. Remove the queen or king from our hearts and minds, in our systems and representations, and what would we be free to invent? Remove the monarchy, and you begin to remove the look of a certain class, the English nobility that no longer reflects the diverse appearances of our country. Such an abolition would remind us that the monarchies which still exist in Europe (in Spain and Denmark) are indigenous. Ours is absentee, marked by occasional grand tours. The end of monarchy might uproot us, and further shake loose our spiritual restlessness, already on the edge of surging. The symbolism once attached to royalty and nobility, the emblems of chivalry, dignity, philanthropy, service, courageous protectiveness, would be revealed to thrive where they were always meant to be—in and through each of us. The true queens and kings: ourselves.

*

Forward in an advanced search:

The fascination with royalty is surely with the glamour of images. "All eyes will be fixed on you," Empress Maria Theresa said to her daughter, Marie Antoinette. Royals carry special status and codes of performance in their appearances. We have obliged, over the centuries, with an attraction to their artificial veils. The Queen, and her family, provided special spectacles for Canadians, a sway of nostalgia and, at times, of solace during wars. Their orderly opulence provided the mystique of solidity. But the e-media has closed in on them, stalking, fixating, zooming in, collecting and gathering images that (perhaps viewers hope) will reveal something, or anything, behind the concealments of pomp and circumstance.

Stephen Frears's *The Queen* and Sofia Coppola's *Marie Antoinette* appeared in cinemas in 2006. Both films show us the power of the royalist image, and the absorption of aristocratic castes with decorum and style. Frears's *The Queen*, beautifully written and acted, is poignant in its intelligible portrait of royalty under siege. It portrays the royal crisis over the death of Princess Diana with documentary-like realism, draining images of sumptuousness, rendering the story almost matter-of-fact, to allow the actors, Helen Mirren most impressively, to shine through, and to let the script's wit and irony play. Coppola's *Marie Antoinette*, albeit about another kind of aristocracy, revels in orgies of candy and champagne. The film evokes an exalted mall of mirrors, with a dazed doll at its clueless core. She drowsily drifts from one ceremonial costuming (or stripping) to another lavish dinner, from one pointless stroll in the gardens to another round of gossip with courtiers. The movie is at its most feverish and hallucinatory when intoxicated by extravagance. History barely obtrudes on the shimmering excess of a phantasmagoric Versailles. Frears's film also offers images of an isolated heroine, Elizabeth II, but her tragedy is to be the only intelligent person in the privileged manors and halls. She believes she must uphold the past, and present a precise image of tact.

Ritual and privacy were to be regally maintained by Elizabeth II, and rigidly separated. In both films violence and death crash the decorative surfaces—the Revolution in *Marie Antoinette*, a smashed-up car in *The Queen*. Style and decorum do not hold out against rage and grief. Each film illuminates how people can be caught in glamour's allure, and in the illusions of status. The films show heroines so remote from their times and places that any encounter with extraordinary events is a shock. They live in palatial worlds that are meant to hover above things (one of the hierarchical imperatives of royalty), and yet imprison them in a cruel quaintness.

Let us say it is ironically fitting that it took two movies to remind us how royalty is now more about surface images than about living symbolism. They show figures vital only when they are dressed up. Theirs is the vertical plane without substance, in decay; the horizontal plane is more often than not a nuisance, sometimes a tragic intrusion. The mythic depths only come with death.

We thus see fascination but little transcendental mystique. This is because the metaphysical intensities of royalty have been drained away. And what we are left with are show, and gossip, and habit, and those codes of performance that belong to ages when people were not to look within, to themselves. The images reveal the shock of emptiness.

*

In *The Human Cycle*, Sri Aurobindo wrote of the mythic phases in the unfolding of identity. There would be ages ruled by castes, inherited rights. Then there would be desperate ages, boiling over with terrifying chaos. He said there must be confusion, even furor, before a mystic integration can occur, or recur. In his evocations of the ages of human civilization, Aurobindo described what was for him the most profound juncture—the subjective stage, the time of the I. This would be the age of self-agency, passionate self-awareness; we would invent the forms we would serve, and we would stop letting forms and structures rule us.

Aurobindo was not referring to the eighteenth-century industrial age view of individualism. This was the concept of the self as a commodity, to be bartered off for better wages. Nor was he referring to the narcissistic self, familiar to us in entertainment culture. He was directing us towards pure subjectivity—the solitudes of identity. This must burn through from unrest. He knew, however, that during the cycle of chaos (similar to the image of unravelling, or spinning, that Yeats gives us in the first stanza of "The Second Coming"), a pall would come over us. We would sense that life was darkening, narrowed by powers we thought that we couldn't directly influence. He had the faith that new defining shapes would arrange themselves like fine filings around magnetic poles, like dew on a rose petal.

The debate about the abolition of the monarchy would be another sign of rising subjectivity. It would become part of the spiritual cycle: to know, lucidly, and intimately, the value of each person's soul, paradoxically independent and interdependent, finite in its physical manifestations, infinite in its capacity to mold consciousness. Royalty is an inappropriate geometry for our restlessness, for the struggling and questioning subjectivity that is the heart of enlarging mind, in our planetary and cosmic affair.

This debate has been brewing for years among citizens. Yet we've been timid about pushing the Canadian proposition on into its obvious, volatile fields. "Above the American Left and Right is Canada, a place free of the American Dream and the European Nightmare," William Irwin Thompson said in *At the Edge of History*. Perhaps it is time to think beyond left and right, and to begin to include thinking in terms of up and down, on the ladder of longing, of heart and mind. Sometimes we can feel this yearning in the scurry and peeves of our elections. Yet the peevishness may also be sensitivity, on the cusp of becoming keen. It may be a discontent with the ways we are addressed and bombarded in terms and concepts we know to be already far behind us. In the e-cosmos all things are sending and receiving. There is perpetual reaction, and response. We have become an ache. But then this is how the cosmos has always been; it is just much more so now. In elections, part of the ceremonial and ritual events of the global amphitheatre, it often appears that people will say what they are against more often than they will say what they are for. A trial of ideas must bring vision. In that debate we could begin to deliver ourselves more to ourselves.

*

Pierre, I believe (revising Yeats) that the age of religious orthodoxy and theoretical rigidities is about to pass, or about to be subsumed, and an age of moods, of inspirations, of high emotion, of the source, of metaphysics, of hybrids, of apocalypse, will take their place. The recognition of other worlds, sensual and super-sensual, is close; this must enlarge our comprehension of rights and the audacities of personhood. The standard of reality will be (and probably already is) symbols, dreams, images, apparitions, and energy traces—the warming of souls; this means that no standard will be immediately palpable.

All portends (or may portend), liberally, that the Universal Spirit will be moving across our senses, through our news, across our screens, into our experiences—over our skin and nerves—brushing up against us, leaving us torn and avid. The spiritual tracking will move faster, and faster, in pressings and intensities difficult—if not impossible—to elude.

In 1941 you wrote to Camille Corriveau, "These different circumstances cause me to envelop myself in a world apart, where I crazily read and wrote, and dreamt about music and beauty and revolutions and blood and dynamite. It was most contradictory this combined desire of action and thought."

When you whirled away behind the Queen in what seemed like a jest, you had learned that an image could be dynamite.

*

Thus when VIA train 638 travelled to Montreal, it crossed provincial borders and linguistic lines, and then crossed over into our imaginations, where the symbol of the rose, and the fire of a calling, were entwined into our national psyche.

IV

SUBSTANCE, PRESSURES, BEYOND
PULSE IN MATTER

Remember that what pulls the strings is within—
hidden from us. Is speech, is life, is the person.

MARCUS AURELIUS

The soul is a sphere in equilibrium. . . . Not fragmenting
outward, not sinking back on itself, but ablaze with
light and looking at the truth, without and within.

MARCUS AURELIUS

Inward Pressure

In Trudeau's *Against the Current: Selected Writings, 1939–1966* we find a rare acknowledgment of his spirituality. He answers the interviewer's query "Are you a believer?" with a simple "Yes." Then: "Let's say . . . I remain . . . a believer." In 1977, in a TV interview with Alain Stanké, he said, "I believe in eternal life, and so I believe in God."

In the book the statement is isolated, and terse. Neither aphorism nor maxim, it's just a statement, simplified (we won't say honed) to the point of a curt announcement. What surrounds the published fragment is elliptical space.

He left such spaces for us. We will not find much anywhere else on soul, or faith, on metaphysics, or mysticism. In his published writings we find many critiques of the oppressiveness of the Catholic Church. On the deep subject of his faith, however, he remained (once more) rigorously evasive. Senator Jacques Hébert said his close friend Trudeau possessed "spiritual strength." McCall and Clarkson in their biography invoke his "spiritual intensity," and then appear to be baffled by what this might mean. He chose to keep this side of himself mostly cloaked. Perhaps more disclosures from his archived papers will draw back that cloak. What we have now are inferences, and the evidence of his actions.

Can we say that his spirit was vivid?

Let us look. His oratory, his persistent articulations of his destiny, his agenda of difference and otherness to be established through minority rights (bilingualism, multi-culturalism) and the culture of the Charter, his conflicts with fellow charismatic Quebeckers, René Lévesque and Lucien Bouchard, were steeped in the cosmopolitan drama, the language of vision. When he died, critics and analysts said that he was an original, "a man of convictions," as if these qualities must make him stand out. *The necessity of Canada, the urgencies of our actions, a just society, the first principle of rights*: these words fired his speeches, and often inflamed our responses.

The soul's flow—call this the current of spirituality in him—can never be wholly invisible. I submit (again) that it is what moved him, and often moved us. It is the spiritual intensity that engages me.

*

I confess that I find mysticism difficult to address. It's hard to write about what is private—and it was to Trudeau—and yet essential to how some endure. Spirituality, faith, the soul's imperative, transcendental concern, immanent experience; one could blunder on to those frontiers. How easy it is to misconstrue the inner bidding. Given one may be living, in parts of Canada and the United States, more and more in a climate of literalist evangelism, one risks being lumped into the camps of reactionary politics and anti-intellectual barbarism.

Yet one may be driven to find words for what seems unsayable, and to come up close to the ineffable. If we perceive that each of us is in a perpetual communion of mystery and mind, then a host of understandings must follow. Thus I wander onto the vertical or esoteric plane—the spirit domain—that continues to shake, blast, bless, knock, inspire, confound, displace and transfigure the horizontal plane, in this case, the realm of political engagement.

In contemporary discourse and debate there is an identification of most spiritual discussion with political reaction and extremism. But look closely at political progressives. Many were moved by the inner necessity. They heeded the callings of the higher self. The most formidable critics of oppression and repression (political and psychological), of the denial of the right to find a personal path, of authoritarianism, of racism, of social inertia and blind obedience to the status quo, of crippling rote, of economic inequality, have often been writers and activists rooted in the unfurling of spirituality on the material plane. Let us assemble a list: John Locke (adapting his idea of innate rights from Thomas Aquinas), Rousseau, Thomas Jefferson, Tolstoy, Martin Luther King Jr., Mahatma Gandhi, Thomas Merton; the visionary company of poets from Milton through to Blake and the American transcendentalists Emerson, Thoreau, Whitman, Harriet Beecher Stowe, the vagabond beats Henry Miller and Allen Ginsberg. Tolerance and justice for them were part of the sacred destiny for creation.

Jefferson's first draft for the Declaration of Independence, written in June 1776, sounded mystic tonalities, "We hold these truths to be sacred & undeniable; that all men are created equal & independent, that from that equal creation they derive rights inherent & inalienable. . . ." John Adams and Benjamin Franklin advised Jefferson to replace "sacred & undeniable" with "self-evident truths." Jefferson was likely a deist, certainly a dissenter who vigorously opposed religious orthodoxy, any power that interfered with what he understood to be the noble and destined progress of radical inwardness. Liberty, equality of opportunity, the valuing of the person, rights—these were self-evident values. Yet any first-year student could tell you that "inalienable rights" and the self-evident premise are more passionate assertions than argument. The so-called common-sense proposition seems barely logical. Are these propositions facts? Are they necessary myths? Yet people shed blood over these words. They strike into the heart. An intuitive knowledge flickered, and often blazed, at the core of the visionaries, in the inspired eyes that seared into their moment. Metaphysical rebelliousness inspired them to ask us to imagine how we could live, and why we should be committed to (yes, devoted to) lifting and transforming our hearts and minds, intensifying and illuminating consciousness, creating conditions where we and our epochs could widen into receptivity and thus into an openness to innovation and breakthrough.

*

1998.

Only once did the subject of Trudeau's faith come up in our conversations.

September in Montreal.

We were talking over our meal at the Chrysanthemum about the Trudeau Era Conference. He noted the involvement of Michael Higgins, then dean of Theology at St. Jerome's College at the University of Waterloo. Higgins intended to discuss Trudeau's faith and its influencing charge on his politics.

Trudeau sat back abruptly, and said vehemently,

"At last."

He didn't say anything more about this, and I didn't press him. It was another of those moments when something opened and then closed. Still I recognized how much spirituality meant to him by the fervour with which he uttered those two words.

Let us recall that his unfinished doctoral thesis was on the interplay between Christianity and socialism. I wonder what this work might have yielded to that restless mind. Then there were his encounters with two mystics. Trudeau met Mounier only once, according to the Nemnis; and according to John English, he had only one direct encounter with Teilhard de Chardin. I wonder what might have come from close conversations with the author of the Personalist Manifesto, who said in a pointed paradox, "We must find our way out of inwardness in order to sustain that inwardness." Was it Mounier's writings and thought that helped to inspire Trudeau to seek communications between citizens, each possessing a unique opportunity for being, across the barriers of poverty and despair? If he did encounter Teilhard, then he would have absorbed the idea of the globe opening like the circle of an eye, becoming a thought and a heartbeat, the power and pulse of consciousness seeking the rapport that forms a "natural telepathy" (McLuhan).

Here is Frye in his notebooks musing on mysticism,

> [It] is being initiated in the mysteries. The mysteries historically were rebirth experiences . . . central to spiritual life . . . [It] takes one from the world of convention and tradition that's always sure it's going somewhere into the inner world of before birth and after death and thrownness and vision.

But surely Trudeau knew that to raise the idea of the sacred, to speak the word "justice" (the key to the cosmos, Thomas Merton said), to raise the challenge of the calling, to raise the possibility that the universe is a *sacra pagina*, so a process that attends to our prayers ("Prayer is reversed thunder," George Herbert said), to raise the idea that liberty is part of our soul's gift, and we could sound like we're about to join a Pat Robertson crusade. Import spirituality into a discussion, and you could sound maddened, like a budding religious fanatic with an agenda of contempt for pluralism and the division of powers between church and state.

Further, invest political debates with spirituality, and we could sound like a past member of President George W. Bush's morning Bible meetings at the White House. During Gulf War Two, the parish priest at Christ Church Anglican in Stouffville said that he wanted to add a prayer to the service for its victims. He meant the babies shredded by cluster bombs. Yes, some parishioners said; but only if he included a prayer for Bush's plans to detonate

Armageddon in the Middle East, following the prophecies in the Book of Daniel. (Bush was, by all reports, especially fond of that book of the Bible.) This would aid in fulfilling the messianic message of a final apocalypse in Jerusalem, and thereby clear the way for the second coming of Jesus. The parish priest politely demurred. (I hoped that Bush's morning readings would move on to Ecclesiastes. Proverbs would have done.)

We must emphasize the difference between spirituality and religious dogma. There is, it seems, an unbridgeable chasm between the concerns of a Sri Aurobindo and a Pat Robertson. Yet enter the cruxes of spirit and matter, cross over into a receptivity to revelation, revive the seeds of destiny, intersect with the language of the sacred, speak of inspiration and miracle, and you could be identified with literalist evangelism, the platitudes of mainstream churches, the paranoia of cults, the willed mindlessness of those who crave the hard certitudes of paternal authority. Certainty is usually a sign of pathology. Worse for a writer, you would likely be called regressive, an upholder of oppressive power structures, or a faddish follower of New Age mistiness. Neo-Marxist theorists will be antagonistic. Secular-minded friends and kindly family members will become grim. All this counsels you to side with Trudeau's near silence on the subject.

But enter spiritual cruxes I must. How else can one set sail and find a horizon?

In *Real Presences*, George Steiner wrote how it's impossible to fully comprehend certain cultural figures without reference to the transcendental. It is notable how some of the most illustrious liberal thinkers—say, John Locke, or Thomas Jefferson—were inclined to the spiritual, even if they were resistant to mainstream theology. I'm using the word "liberal" in its radical Latinate source, from *libera*, meaning the free person, who can, and must, make choices. Let us recall, though, how the rigorous nontheist Nietzsche branded subsequent generations of liberals "flatheads." He said this in *Twilight of the Idols* when he condemned George Eliot, and all the followers of John Stuart Mill's liberalism, for shallow proselytizing, so-called "moral fanaticism" or "right thinking." Nietzsche hammered home how the English moralists wanted a good society with freedom of conscience and speech, with protection of the citizen's right to economic fairness, without transcendental reference or justification. This would be decency "emancipated from theology."

Nietzsche thought that Eliot and Mill wanted to have a Christian, soul-based society, without Christ, or the soul. "By breaking one main concept out of it, the faith in God, one breaks the whole," he taunted. "Nothing necessary remains in one's hands." His furious honesty towards Eliot and Mill brings me up short. Examine the punning depths of the phrase "nothing necessary," in Walter Kaufmann's cunning translation of Nietzsche's lines. Can anyone find necessity in "nothing"? Can one speak of faith in humankind without faith in the soul? What gives meaning if we strip away the mystical? Why would the liberals refuse to acknowledge that by denying the spirit they would have decisively broken with the sacred? And why not break with the concept of God entirely? Nietzsche's assault leads one to recognize how certain thinkers evaded spirituality, hiding it behind high-minded abstractions. Let's continue this observation: a thinker or writer, an activist or philosopher, may drop spirituality altogether from reference because they wish to evade the inference, and the enormity, of the beyond, and the complex implications of including it. That fear of appearing like a mystagogue following missionary tracks and obscure reveries could be very great.

We can see how it might become impossible for some to explain the urgency of their first principles, and what the source of the pressures and crystallizations may be. Return then to metaphor, or poetry—to fragment, and ellipse. Let the gaps and silences speak, and leave enigmas behind like traces in dust. Bend with the wind, be a "thinking reed" (Pascal).

If we can't see the imperatives of the spirit in explanations, then we may find it in actions.

Look at Trudeau's political imagination, actions, style and will. Here was a statesman drenched in the spirituality of confirming the rights and potential of personhood through the Charter, of witnessing (and altering) history through wholehearted existential engagement, of demanding that we pursue what is best in us, of recognizing that words and speeches, public ritual and gesture carry intention and allusion, of seeing what is inescapable in our lives, of finding a unity with other souls in our essential engagements, thus to fight at every turn the alienating agonies of separation.

The word "cosmos" inhabits "cosmopolitanism." The political battles waged in Canada were a microcosm of universal charges: rights, a just use of resources and materials, the opportunity to find employment, protection of the interior way and so of difference, the importance of government to encourage and provide for personhood, and the limitations of the state over inward evolutions.

*

In *A Farewell to Arms*, Ernest Hemingway bitterly wrote about how soldiers became suspicious of bloated abstractions like "justice." In *Darkness at Noon*, Arthur Koestler showed how people under Communism were murdered in the name of "the future." Too many people have been butchered on behalf of so-called higher truths. After the ruthless introduction by political leaders of the concept of "preemptive war," we are justified in our suspicions of what they mean when they invoke "liberty." Great gulfs exist in the meanings of these words.

Never in my years of talking to Trudeau did I sense that he thought the words were campaign slogans. They were open to interpretation, points of ambiguous reference, surely. A practiced tactician will proverbially announce that the "the future is what matters." Such statements by politicians are seldom nuanced. But we may reflect with Trudeau that the experience of these words was more than clichéd. The need to persuade us of their necessity lifted him, and sometimes ourselves, into acknowledging that we could be more than we have been; and that our destiny was not to merely waffle, or to blindly welcome every initiative, but to reason out constantly how we may differ.

This is why our place and time for Trudeau remained such a beautiful possibility. Despite the mistakes and confusions, the weaknesses and flaws, of a political life where disappointment is inevitable and policy is transitory, Canada herself was a context of beauty. Someone with visionary heart knows that "beauty" is no mere ornament.

Beauty is part of the idea of harmony. It conjures awe, and the awful terror of the new. It speaks to the infinite variety in our engagements. Beauty evokes purposefulness, rather than design—spontaneous eruptions, joy in forms for their own sake. Things are beautiful when they are truly alive. Energy rejoices in itself, paraphrasing Blake.

"The ancient Greeks called the world . . . beauty" (Emerson). It is an operation of the sublime, restoring a sense of causes, and of cause, putting us on the cusp of deep perception. "We are never tired, so long as we can see far enough" (Emerson). We find harmonies in the shapely cut of a finely wrought sentence, in the overtones of a word, in the way water ripples behind a gliding canoe, in the glow of our lover's eyes, in the vulnerability in our children's faces, in the way our lives navigate currents and waves.

Beauty, like loving, sometimes seems a kind of crisis. It brings us to the crossroads and thresholds of the perpetual choosing. Immediacy thus impels us.
　The recognition of beauty is part of the soul's flow.

*

Reflect on this: Trudeau was a creature of the 1960s, a period when electric mass media and progressive politics, when new technologies and financial abundance, briefly converged. The hopeful world-pulse was heightened, and impelling. The spiritual shift surrounded us, tingeing and encoding us with cryptic promises of dawn. "I want History to jump on Canada with sharp skates" (Leonard Cohen).

I was too young to go to Woodstock, but old enough to understand the longing in its songs and cries for peace. Joni Mitchell lamented in "Woodstock" how we were stardust, golden, but caught in an evil bargain, with the warmth of paradise—"*the garden*"—calling to us. This was her apocalyptic take on the moment's meaning. (She sang the song in a drifting, poignant style on her album *Ladies of the Canyon*, but didn't perform at the concert herself.)

In 1968 Trudeau had the aura of heretical youth. (He was in fact already in his late forties.) This was a mask he eventually shed to become the mentoring parent for a constitutionally renewed country.

But early on I sensed, with others, that if Trudeau became Prime Minister, there would be a chance for Canada to leap ahead. It could become a place primed for the planetization of culture and technology that McLuhan described: multiform and protean, and expanded by vivid metamorphoses. Society's forms would be at the service of personality. A restored communication with spirit would break with the cold status quo of impersonal structures.

Events of our youth forever guide us.

I bumped into Trudeau in the jostling crowds on the floor of the Liberal convention in Ottawa in 1968. He was being hurried away by his aides after he'd given his speech. I had no chance to speak to him. His speech had been calm and eloquent, but it had by no means been the fieriest of the night. That honour belonged to John J.

("Joe") Greene, one of the leadership candidates, who gave a memorable rabble-rouser.

My father had taken me to the convention. He often took me to important occasions. Powe Sr. worked for John Turner during the race, so over the days we were there I had to secretly pin my Trudeau buttons to the inside of my jacket.

Although Trudeau's speech had not shown him at his peak, I shared with the people gathered there a sense of the momentous. He became leader, after four ballots. His wave to the crowd after his victory—a gesture caught in many photographs—seemed to be at once a signal to the airwaves and a beckoning to the future. We felt the nearness of dreams, the world turning towards the new.

But violence shadowed the victory.

Martin Luther King Jr. had been gunned down weeks before. American cities smouldered. Troops and tanks guarded the White House. Weeks later, in June, Robert Kennedy was murdered, after his California primary victory, in the kitchen of an L.A. hotel. On the nightly TV news we saw the napalm horror of Vietnam. The mood could turn savage, and cruel, with hints of insurrections to come.

The feverish atmosphere infiltrated us. Recall the scene: On June 24, at that St. Jean Baptiste Day celebration in Montreal we saw Trudeau on TV sitting with dignitaries in front of the *bibliothèque municipale*. In night images we watched psychic tensions burst out. The extremist wings of the separatist movements had found their target, and tossed bottles at the stands, some filled with acid, some with kerosene. The moment was on the verge of conflagration.

We saw him resist the urgings of bodyguards to leave. What kept him there we will never know. Impressions of the night imprinted us. They showed grim-faced police aligned in darkness. In ironic contrast, others showed smiling costumed angels waving from floats. Authority and spirit; it was as if at that parade, and during the riot, the shocking zeniths and nadirs of the time were exposed. When we look deeply into the images of Trudeau and the rioters, we see premonitions of the War Measures Act: he would be the opponent of those who would incite revolutionary upheaval. While he stayed still in the maelstrom, he was probably seething within; he was capable, we would learn, of retaliation.

The riot in the street must have bruised him more than we understood. His sensitivity to moods and aspirations, to the climate of the moment and the wound of frustrated ambition, may have alerted him to the knowledge that swiftly coming down upon us all would be the obsessive conviction of ideologues who could suddenly turn from political reform to terrorism. The rage to change was about to go too far.

*

The allure of the extraordinary hovered in the air. If the soul was rising, so was the countering force. There was Romanticism reborn—when it seemed that the renewing spirits of Blake, of the Wordsworth we knew in the "Intimations" ode, of Shelley's prophetic blasting West Wind, of Whitman's celebration of the Self, were sparking again in the feedback wail of electric guitars and the lyrical push of rock and folk—and there was the damper of law and order, the suppressive need to control liberty. Unruly energies would be met by mistrust and caution. In the moods of the 1960s and early '70s we felt the vacillations between ecstasy and the hunger for vision, and dread and the demand for authority.

Trudeau lived inside the rages of liberty and repression—an eternally conflicted place.

On those streets that night we witnessed a war of wills, epic and epochal. He was an advocate of personal excellence, who would promote incendiary dialogues about rights. He was also the guardian who would not budge if he thought that the seething in the streets threatened to overturn peace and law. He had an intimate knowledge of extremism because he had tried to ride in himself the duelling energies of metaphysical imperative and political expedience.

When he retired in 1984, and entered the periods of silence and reflection, he found his last role. He could no longer return to being a rebel, but he could be the elder, livid enough to speak outside the channels of governing.

In this period he came again to challenge the structures and forms of power.

*

Figures that compel the imagination rarely appear in politics. I doubt if Trudeau could be elected in any election now. Tom Axworthy (Trudeau's principal secretary from 1981 to 1984) told me that he doubted if any politician in that mould could have been elected after 1972. Nor can I imagine anyone in the United States electing the introspective Jefferson. Many politicians feel the pulse of the inward pressure. Yet the relentless battering by religious lobby groups, who demand that leaders represent their highly specific agendas, could make many political aspirants nurture the silence of self-restraint. The visionary impulse could be turned to the quiet trust that people will find their way, and that democracies must offer a multitude of choices, not the confining programs determined by a restrictive group claiming sole custody of truth.

Should we fear charismatic leaders? Is there something in us that makes us shy away from public intensities and the call to eminence? "The problem with socialism is that it is too dull; the problem with fascism is that it is too exciting," Susan Sontag once quipped. Her memorable comment becomes even more pointed when we deal with charismatic beings, and those often confounding intersections of soul and matter.

I submit, nevertheless, that charisma and metaphysics are inextricably linked. Inspiration and conviction combined can become audacity in the public realm. If one feels questioned by the cosmos, and if one questions the cosmos back, then one must be driven on. We may come to prefer our leaders bland because this promises a degree of predictability. But then we come again to this conundrum: if there is no appeal to the eternal, and to whatever pulls us beyond the concerns of power and management, then that appeal often appears empty. We feel a void, and mask our responses in indifference and suspicion.

*

If transcendence is the soul urging us to go beyond the confines of our inherited notions of identity, then immanence is the recognition that sacred energies abide in all events and matter. We see the transcendental drive in the hunger of personality to break free of stereotypes, away from boundaries. We find immanence in the e-milieu of surge and blackout.

And e-media Mysteries amplify and reel around us. Images from Gulf War Two harrowed us in 2003. They continue to shower us, and dislocate us, from the tsunami in Southeast Asia in 2004 to the drowning of New Orleans in 2005. The e-cosmos clings to us like static around wires. The secret of the soul in this stream of communications is the point where our inner worlds and the discarnate fuel of electricity touch. It is then we become more than the existential I, and closer to the transcendental I that Novalis said is the goal of all quests: the instant when we each become both one and many, echo and depth.

"We can't perceive any of these energies without instruments, so most people don't realize how drastically and abruptly we've changed the electromagnetic environment in just one century," Robert O. Becker wrote, with Gary Selden, in *The Body Electric: Electromagnetism and the Foundation of Life*. Emblems and apparitions rush and flow, in event clusters, and in these radiating fields we feel the ceaseless networks of transmissions. We are reminded of sorrow and survival, and the images recall and visualize our power, which we see is titanic. At any time we may be pulled into the world's pain and beauty. "Skillful we are in propelling messages and bombs," Trudeau said in 1970.

Is electricity the fabled *prima materia* of the alchemists? The *prima materia* was the unconscious waters for C.G. Jung; it was chaos for Julia Kristeva.

Simultaneously never has institutional authority seemed so successfully codified. Never has "the system" appeared more monstrous and remote from the touch of citizens.

Worlds surge into us, at the flick of a TV or VDT switch, empowering the user. Meanwhile information blindly trembles, fluid and mutable, without a personal imprint. Government, corporations, universities, big business media, all rule by doctrine, system, code, structure, bottom-line figures. I have heard students say how troubled they are by how institutions, even their own schools, seem immune to their longings and inspirations, often dismissive of the narrative of the meaningful quest. And at once access to the workings of power has never been greater than through the Web.

We hover in the *prima materia* opening, and yet we ask, How open are our lives and times? How can we each be read?

It is hard to know the soul's temperature may rise in conditions where we may feel involved and shunted aside. What often seems to be slouching towards us is a massive reinstated Leviathan, imposing dispirited repressions, and irresolution, born over and over in the Bethlehem of our living rooms and workspaces, through the screens we've set out for ourselves in looped images, nightmares where it asserts its reign through fatigue and psychosomatic illnesses, and all the vexations of hopelessness.

*

Pierre, this is what I've learned from the conversations that haven't ended.

Drain the debate about why we're here from glimmers of the eternal and we could reduce our premises to mechanics. Cover the cruxes of spiritual longing with purely material concerns and we may be left with rote and convention. Excuse notions of quest and excellence, and we're left with more answers than questions. If we replace metaphysical biddings with messianic ideology (with certitude and dogma) then the results will be horrible, so we witnessed in the violence of the last century, and we witness in the terrorist extremism of ours. We always travel along the razor's edge, but without that edge we numb ourselves to call and calling, its risks, and its elevations.

You spoke of a just society. After the War Measures Act in 1970, you appeared to abandon the idea. People often criticized you for this. During the constitutional debates of the early 1980s it seemed to be what kept you returning to the conference table. You brought the phrase back in the 1990s, once you'd been out of power, and you felt free to once more express what was closest to you. By then a just society had become this in your mind: the perpetual re-creation of conditions that would respect the fire in each of us, and allow that fire to burn peacefully, in the pluralist process.

What did you try to pass on in the end? Search all you can for connection. When you find connection, cherish it. We should create climates in which choices and meanings multiply. Look for guides, and learn to do without them.

Let data flow, and don't be afraid of how it may spin us around. Remember that here, now, is privileged, a place where the psychic fires can burn, and where we can find the solitude and space to review our actions and choices.

I've been teaching myself how to read between the lines, and into images, then into symbols.

Pierre, the most striking of all the implications that have emerged from contemplating your actions and words is this: enlightenment should be a human right.

*

I doubt if it's romanticizing to say that Trudeau kept his spirituality private because his words and actions revealed his heart. He didn't have to express directly what was obvious in his dramas. To our motto of "Peace, Order, and Good Government," with its overtones of subjugation and prohibition, he added the Charter's emphasis on personal rights, and therefore on degrees of liberty, and ultimately on the inward pressure. In this reading of his actions, we may understand the still-controversial War Measures Act in terms of the protection of the rights of the general populace against the vicious extremism of a fanatical few. The application of the act, often indiscriminately punitive, is another question. He affirmed through the Charter his alliance with the line of visionaries who felt the inner pulse and articulated how the soul must flow. Our most solitary of Prime Ministers allowed his sense of imperative, and his contradictory metamorphoses of personality, to be transparent.

And how do we air what is essential, and yet private, in the vertigo of the imagery spin and spell of the e-cosmos? What would a calling of first principles mean, even if this must be left unspoken, a trace to be intuited?

I suggest this:

It means to know our names have individual shape and potentially a destiny (not a mere fate); to remember how powerful we are and can be (the power to murder and create); to love the world which is our paradise; to remind one another that we are beings of inherent value and beauty (even when this seems most obscured from our view); to listen for vestiges of seemingly lost harmonies (Shakespeare reminded us, through Lorenzo's speech in *The Merchant of Venice*, Act V, Scene I, that this was the fabled music of the spheres); to know that we are engaged with what is here because we must be; to chart ourselves back into the enwombing outlines of the source that encompasses—and compasses—our minds and souls.

Metaphysical Glances

. . . "Reckless, O soul, exploring, I with thee, and thou with me . . ." Trudeau quoted Whitman's poetry in a 1946 letter to Thérèse Gouin.

The lines, from "Passage to India," ecstatically envision a mental pilgrimage into territories of the Spirit. Whitman's title and poem (in the fifth, 1870 edition of *Leaves of Grass*) framed E.M. Forster's fiction about a passage East, into mysterious conjunctions. It framed David (*Lawrence of Arabia*, *Dr. Zhivago*) Lean's last film about what happens to high spiritual sensibilities when they find themselves in blunting conflicts and the impoverishment of closed political and cultural systems.

. . . Do not overlook Trudeau's yoga training (which he sometimes used for stunts). It increases will and determination. Yoga conditions the body and prepares the senses to be open to influential energies, greater than the confines of background and tradition. He travelled East in 1948, and by train, boat, car and foot, went from Eastern Europe, to Israel, Iraq, India, Kashmir, then on to Thailand, French Indochina (Vietnam), and China, and Japan. He saw brigands, wars of separation, disease, corruption. We have yet to fully grasp what he absorbed. No person returns from such travels unmarked. "It was my destiny to join in a great experience.... I was permitted to be a participant in a unique journey" (Hermann Hesse).

... What Trudeau learned from his experiences crossing borders, exposed to mentors like John Kenneth Galbraith who were "citizens of the world": if racial identity, the blood-ties of nationality, become the dominant business of the state, tyranny is not far off.

... One could pick politics to enact a destiny. Politics could then become a metaphor for the evolutions of identity. The good itself then becomes a quest (Simone Weil).

... "The human person has a transcending social significance" (Trudeau, 1970).
... "People who criticized me used to say that I was Protestant more than a Catholic because I like to impose constraints on myself, but I don't like them to be imposed from the outside" (Trudeau, 1971).

... Think out loud to indicate the edges of thought. These edges may become points that pierce through the hide and places of fear. They are also like waves that reveal more underneath: protean change.
... Shun connectives if you wish to speak in startling suggestions. Above all, startle yourself, with lacunae.

. . . The maxim "Go to the people, and ask them" is a trusting recognition that people will seek truths, if asked to do so.

. . . "With text messaging everyone can receive the call." An overheard remark.

. . . Evolutionary democracy is preferable to revolutionary societies because it allows the process of individual warming and global nearness to coincide. We embrace cosmopolitanism over economic globalization, Genesis over Armageddon.

. . . Keep Canada from becoming an empire—or, if possible, a mere outpost of other empires (British, continental French, American).

. . . The striving to be cosmopolitan can become a deliberate process of exile.

"Exile contains redemption within itself, as seed contains the fruit" (a Kabbalist saying).

. . . Let us acknowledge that you may begin one way at the start of the journey, and another (wholly) at the end.

. . . After you start, you may stand around with fragments in your hands.

. . . If dynamism is the model, then ideas, like nature, must evolve. We are moving away from massive singularity. No stasis, but emergence—observation, absorption, reception, strange breakdowns—a constant sensing of vibrations (you are what you can bear).

. . . Every drama, in politics or otherwise, is potentially mythical, an experience in depth, a drawing of your own face through the meeting with what you supposed is destiny.

. . . The pilgrim at the end of the day returns to himself and finds this—his face—is what has been emerging all along.

. . . Each of us part of a perpetual scrolling, or writing, or inscribing, or image formation. There are innumerable readings. No person or group has final say. Each authentic (strong or weak) interpretation is true enough, to the reader and the reading, the user and the scanning.

Your version—of Trudeau, of anything—comes next.

Turning

I've been circling around Trudeau in the process of asking questions, enlarging on ideas and images, creating and re-creating, moving towards knowing more. The pattern behind the moments is identity, and its urgencies and progress towards what may become the visionary moment. In remembering and reinvention the soul grows.

The soul doesn't follow a predetermined plot line, however. It expands and contracts, like breathing. The sphere of the soul hovers, rests, cycles forward, stops, starts, wobbles, cracks, loses its track, comes together, matures, comes to quietness and then begins again.

In endless rotation events, people, things, thoughts, become a matter of nuance. We see subtleties and shadings. There is thus much more (worlds within worlds) when we go round and reflect again. We see there is no end to the process, its magnetic and provocative wave, embodying contraries and complexities, breaks like accidents, and perplexity. The circle nevertheless widens. The sphere of attention is also a pulse.

Circling brings repetition, but the cycle is never exactly the same. Repetition is reinforcement, and part of the perpetual attempt to get closer to the unidentifiable centre. (A circle is only a frame for the inexpressible, a bank for the source that flows without form.)

Meditation involves circling, the deepening of the mind when focused on a pattern. A mandala is sometimes called an enigma. We may focus the circles of our attention on a form of nature (a rose, a willow tree, a river current, a leaf of grass, a star in the night sky), on the forms of our invention (a word, a book, a TV, a computer screen, a wire, a camera, a telephone), on the persona of a fictional character, on the personality of one we thought we knew.

*

1987.
    In his office at Heenan Blaikie on de Maisonneuve.
    It was the day that I brought books.
    I had handed him a page with a passage that I'd typed up from Erich Fromm's *The Anatomy of Human Destructiveness*.

> . . . reason is more than intelligence; it develops only when the brain and the heart are united, when feeling and thinking are integrated, and when both are rational . . . The loss of the ability to think in terms of constructive visions is in itself a severe threat to survival.

"That's fascinating. Exactly what I've tried to express for years," he said. "Reason shapes passion. Not thinking without passion. The press hasn't always understood what I meant by this. I like the quotation very much. May I keep it?"
    Of course, I told him.

"Reason and passion together. That's what I meant. A rational person has all this in balance."

(The ratio or harmony of the senses, I thought to myself.)

He added, in what sounded to me like an afterthought that even surprised him,

"Violence is the last refuge of people with nothing left to say."

I pointed to the books I'd placed on his desk.

"Well, you certainly have enough here to keep you reading for a month."

"More like a week," he snapped, as if I'd challenged his capacity to concentrate.

Over lunch.

We talked politics and politicians.

"Have you read Chrétien's memoirs, *Straight from the Heart*?" he asked.

"Yes."

"Is it worth reading?"

"Not really."

"Why not?"

He looked ready for a debate.

"He pulls his punches."

"Really?" He smiled. "That means Jean is getting ready to come back to politics." (Chrétien had not yet returned to lead the federal Liberal party.)

"You stayed in politics without pulling your punches a good deal of the time," I said.

"That may be. But I knew early on that many people weren't going to vote for me no matter what I did. So there was no point in trying to appeal to them."

He continued to comment on Chrétien.

"He has strong political instincts. He does, however, need very good people around him. You know, I'd offer Jean a portfolio, and he'd balk and say, 'I can't do that one.' Then he'd go away and think about it. The next day he'd come back and say, 'Yes, I'll do it if I can have so and so as Deputy Minister.' And Jean would invariably pick a first-class character. Well, as long as Jean is being properly briefed by good people, he'll be fine. He's always in the process of . . . educating himself."

We started a conversation about free trade.

"Free trade is a great liberal tradition. After all, Wilfrid Laurier fought an election on its principles, and lost. You could argue that free trade is a challenge to the status quo. There are many industries that simply can't compete in the post-industrial society. You could say the whole strategy for Mulroney . . ."

(Always the scathing edge in his voice for those he opposed. He pronounced "roney" to rhyme with "phony.")

". . . would be to argue it as a challenge. It's a momentous time in our history. The problem is what is *this* deal about? A distinction should be made. The Liberals should be saying we are not for *this* deal. *Better* deals can be negotiated. This isn't being made clear enough."

I brought up Paul Martin Jr.

"He'd make a good manager of the corporate machine. He's ten percent smarter than Mulroney," he said.

*

1989.

At the same restaurant.

"When I was young, around twenty-one or twenty-two," he said, "it was liberty that obsessed me. Liberty was really all that I thought about. There was, of course, at that time an authoritarian mood in Quebec. From the authoritarian church to the corrupt provincial government. They were nets I wanted to throw off."

While I listened to him, I realized how much of what he said resembled what James Joyce had Stephen Dedalus say in *A Portrait of the Artist as a Young Man*. "I shall try to fly by those nets," Stephen declares, invoking his desire to transcend nation, culture, church and family, the binds that inhibited the growth of his imagination. Once Trudeau left Montreal for his education in America and Europe, in the Middle East and in the East, he thought that he was throwing off those binds, too. "Drive your cart and your plow over the bones of the dead," Blake said, in a trenchant maxim from *The Marriage of Heaven and Hell*.

"But when I entered politics," he said, "I changed my mind. I began to feel that equality of opportunity was one of the most important factors in that trinity of liberty, equality and fraternity. Equality of opportunity over the liberty to do anything you wanted. Equality in order to restore justice to the system."

He said this, speaking quietly, in the after-burn of the Reagan, Mulroney, and Thatcher years, and their neo-conservative policies. Though he made no direct reference to them, I knew where he was directing his words.

"I've begun to realize how inequality—I mean inequality of *opportunity*—can be the source of injustice. For if liberty only applies to the privileged and the strong, those who exercise their liberty through will and expense accounts, then their expression of liberty must be oppressive. Who else can afford to be completely free except for the rich?"

He sounded like he was sorting out his ideas. In fact he was preparing a polemic. These thoughts would appear in one of the two contributions he made to the 1990 collection *Towards a Just Society*.

Typically, when he spoke in this way he glared into you. I had the sensation I was being X-rayed. He made slicing gestures with his hands. Yet his voice remained quiet, his tone was steady.

"What if it's only the wealthy that have liberty?" he asked. "The underprivileged, the weak, the desperate, the sick, the elderly, may need equality in society in order to establish justice. Take the current regimes. They give more power to the rich, and liberty to the rich, through tax breaks. What happens to the less privileged?"

He stopped. I could tell by the intent expression on his face that he was reaching into his mind to find the next words.

"Liberty . . ."

He thought more, and then said,

". . . It's still essential to me. But equality of opportunity must be the essence of a just society. This means a constant process of understanding the limits of liberty. If liberty isn't for everyone, then it too can become a tyranny."

When he addressed these large issues, I picked up the tension building in him. And I did ask myself, Who was he trying to persuade? Was it me, or was it himself?

I wasn't sure then (and I'm not sure now) that he was convinced of every aspect of his argument. The inwardness he carried, and cultivated, like a provocation to those who would try to solve an enigma, was (and is) an expression of radical liberty. Personality must always break bindings, and remake forms.

Charismatic beings are often cast in the glow of youthful ardour because they project renewal. Their disturbance of the old order brings on an excess of high expectation. Moreover, private life inspires the intensities of inwardness. Alone thought and imagination go free. Social frames are forsaken for mental expansion. Is this the liberty no others can circumscribe?

*

1990.

At the same restaurant.

I commented on how many people had criticized him for his detachment.

"I never had time to worry much about what people were thinking," he said. "I was too busy. I guess my haughtiness, or whatever you want to call it, protected me. I really didn't care that much. Maybe I should have, but I didn't. I was trying to keep my mind on what was happening."

*

1989.

A lunch at the Beaver Room, in (ironically enough) the Queen Elizabeth Hotel.

"Why did President Reagan order American troops into Grenada?" I recalled that crisis, setting up what I'd hoped would be a witticism.

Trudeau watched warily from across the table. Perhaps he thought I was about to make an uncalled-for pronouncement on foreign policy.

"To make the world safe for Club Med," I said.

He laughed quickly then went on smiling while he processed the joke. Abruptly his demeanour changed. The shift was so rapid that it took me aback. He became grave.

"There's more truth in that than you know," he said.

He concluded his remark with a harsh sigh, like a judgment.

*

1990.

We discussed Joseph de Maistre, the dark apostate of the Enlightenment. De Maistre was the nemesis of the idealism of Voltaire and Diderot. He charged that humankind couldn't endure life without divine sanction. Man alone was brutish. God, de Maistre said, imposed restrictive boundaries through ecclesiastical authority. He argued that God demanded blood sacrifice. The wayward person was too weak to find anything on his own. Fallen personality must be contained through obedience to institutional dogma.

"A strange man for you to be reading," Trudeau said in a fatherly way. It was as if he was concerned that a contamination might seep through de Maistre's critique.

"*Les Soirées de Saint-Petersburg*. I read it many years ago . . . He had an interesting mind. I've never forgotten him. He was the true opponent of what the agents of reason stood for. When I was a boy he was much admired by my teachers. We weren't supposed to admire Voltaire. So, of course, I did. I read everything I could find by Voltaire. I made sure my teachers saw me reading him too."

I told him about Isaiah Berlin's essay "The Crooked Timber of Humanity," in *The New York Review of Books*. Berlin had examined de Maistre's thinking, and posited that he was the forefather of modern authoritarian politics, the avatar of those who thought human beings were fuelled by an unquenchable greed that inevitably leads to violence. Monstrousness was endemic to life according to de Maistre. The heart couldn't be trusted; the mind was prone to delusion. Selfishness and stupidity could only be disciplined and directed, never removed. I took him to be the model for Dostoyevsky's Grand Inquisitor, and (possibly) Judge Holden in Cormac McCarthy's *Blood Meridian*.

"An interesting thesis," he said. This was his way of saying "Continue."

"I've found a curious gap in de Maistre's thinking."

"Which is?"

"The omission of love."

"Love."

He sat back, surprised by that word. He waited for more.

*

1998.

At the Chrysanthemum, in the autumn.

I asked Trudeau about the nature of authority in government. Did he think that people needed a leader? Could the leader sometimes become a bully? Wasn't this the threat of paternal leadership, that it would come to impose, rather than direct? Was democracy a form of government that would one day make such forms of leadership less important than direct citizen engagement?

He was silent for a long time. The silence went on for so long I began to wonder if I'd gone somewhere he didn't want to go.

I reformulated the questions.

Was the need for leadership a sign of mistrust in ourselves? Did the Charter espouse, through implication, the higher callings of self, which would eventually rebel against the idea of final authority?

He seemed to weigh the latent challenge of the questions.

I pressed one more time, asking again.

He looked off, and stared, as if he couldn't, or wouldn't, hear me. I had the impression that he was gritting his teeth. He looked back at me, then at the table. He picked up a plate of steaming shrimp. His hand slightly shaking, he passed it over.

"Shall we talk about this another time?" he said.

He never answered those questions.

*

1990.

"De Maistre elevates authority," I said. "His is the most severe philosophy. It's a more brutal picture of a fallen cosmos than the one you'd find in Hobbes's *Leviathan*."

I was getting wound up, hardly conscious of the fact that I was saying all this to the man who had brought in the War Measures Act, and a temporary suspension of civil rights. I did note that his stare had intensified. He was sitting in an aggressive posture in his chair.

"De Maistre's philosophy is one that acknowledges the power of the irrational over the rational," I said. "But the irrational for him is dangerous. It's the dark line over which we shouldn't cross. He says that human beings are far too vulnerable. Their hearts can't deal with the irrational. All should be left to authority. In this case the church. Yet nowhere in his writings do I find him acknowledging the most mysterious energy in the cosmos. It's the energy that counters the demand for blood sacrifice. That energy is love."

"And Dostoyevsky? How does he fit in here?"

"De Maistre's arguments set the stage for the Grand Inquisitor in *The Brothers Karamazov*. You recall, Ivan Karamazov tells the tale of how the Inquisitor lectures the Messiah on how humans crave safety and bread. They want security. People don't want liberty, the Inquisitor says. They're too afraid of choosing for themselves. Was Dostoyevsky thinking of de Maistre when he wrote that part of his novel?"

"It's a good hypothesis. What was the answer given by the Messiah to the Grand Inquisitor? I've forgotten."

"The Messiah listens quietly to the sermon. When it's done he crosses the floor and embraces the Inquisitor. The Inquisitor asks him to leave mankind alone. They're not ready for his message. And the Messiah leaves, without giving an answer. But Dostoyevsky describes how all through the next days the Inquisitor glows. Doesn't that gesture reveal the other factor in time? Love. Forgiveness. Embracing the other. Embracing life."

He sat forward.

Here was his response. It was unlike anything I'd heard him say before.

"There's something more one could say. More strongly still people are driven by the sense of justice. They are moved by a sense of fairness. From where does the striving for justice come? Why is it there? Why do we fight so hard for such an elusive concept? If we can't get people to love one another, at least for now, then we try to guide them towards being more just. I believe it can be justice that determines relations between people. I find this difficult to dismiss in history. The whole enlightenment program thrives on the sense that we must find a fair arrangement in law and wealth. Against hate, violence and greed, against authoritarianism, we can see justice emerging as a force. Perhaps it's the one element of reason in history, the one force hate can't suppress."

He had been weary that day when we'd come down the elevator from his office, out to the street, around the corner, on to the restaurant. Now he spoke with emotion.

"Do you think the idea of justice comes from feeling or intellect?" I asked.

"It comes from both. We can feel when something is unjust. We know it. And if, as de Maistre says, there are evils in society that no social contract or educational program can remedy or restrain, then why do we find the presence of reason? Why do we find acts of goodness and charity? Why do we do find that sense of outrage if justice isn't done? Why do people strive for more and more fairness in their political systems? Why do people wrestle with the idea of whom or what they will serve? These are more than delusions."

I wondered if the law is the highest we can achieve

without love. The process of law is progress along the horizontal plane. But perhaps love is the process of the vertical plane. It's the flowering of emotion, the trusting of intuition. The fire burns into us. And if you have love, then will you find justice?

"Call it an evolution," I said. "Something moving through time. Instead of revolution maybe we should be talking about awakening. And the evolution of political systems towards democracy will allow the awakening to continue."

We were interrupted by the waiter who brought us the bill.

And it was there that we stopped. But I felt that I was learning a lot, and that there much more to say, and to learn, in other times, in other places.

*

1992.

A telephone call from Montreal.

We talked about the vehement debates that swirled around the Constitution and the issue of unity during the political furor that engulfed the government's Charlottetown Accord, and the referendum on it.

"Do you think Canada will prevail through this? Will we last?" I asked.

"I made a promise to the provinces and to the people during the constitutional debates . . . that each province would be treated equally before the law. Special powers are a legal bind. They mean the road to dissolution."

"But Canada isn't a rigidly unified country, and never will be. Neither multiculturalism nor multilingualism are energies that unite. They create a process, yes. An acceptance of the human range . . ."

"Canada doesn't have to be completely unified, as you put it. We need only agree to continue. The nation, and nationality, should never be an absolute. Remember your Bergson. . . . Creative change. Things move on. The point is, don't stop change by putting us in a bind with these deals."

In a letter to me, dated September 13, 1993, he would reinforce the idea of the flux,

Canada is what it is becoming in the electronic age. Heraclitus . . . all things change and nothing stays. Henri Bergson: the creative evolution.

The Canada you propose is one that my children perceive already, though dimly, and that yours will perceive soon . . .

As ever,
Pierre

*

1987.

We shared a table with Senator Leo Kolber and his wife at the Beaver Room. (Trudeau at his office: "Do you mind if the senator and his wife join us?" I: "Not at all." He: "If you do mind I certainly don't mind cancelling. But if we go with him, we'll go to a very nice restaurant and he'll pay for it.")

The conversation took in the Liberal Party's leadership, and the backroom concerns of politics.

Mrs. Kolber at one point responded to a remark made by Trudeau on style in politicians.

He'd said,

"Mulroney has some style. Turner has none at all."

"Pierre, what you're saying is very enigmatic," she said.

"That's what I intended." He was curt.

A waiter set a basket of buns to my right. In the midst of our talk, I made a grandiose gesture with my right hand and knocked the top bun from the basket, sending it flying across the room. The bun flew over to another table, where it rolled to a halt in front of the mayor of Montreal's plate. The mayor looked bemused. Aghast waiters reared back.

"Oh my God," I said. I felt like an idiot.

When I found the courage to look up, I saw Trudeau busily rearranging his cutlery.

Suddenly he fumbled with his fork. The fork bounced up high into the air and clattered down on the floor. Abruptly several waiters lunged over to help, scrambling down to pick up his fork. Then the spoon bounced up and rattled down.

Appalled waiters hustled around his corner of the table. Trudeau shooed them away, and struggled down to pick up the cutlery. While he did, he so looked awkward, straining towards the floor. Then he popped back up, with an amused glint in his eyes. He looked across the table. The senator and his wife were silent.

Then Trudeau shrugged.

"There seems to be some sort of electromagnetic field here," he said.

After we'd eaten, and talked more, we said goodbye to the senator and to his wife, and thanked them for lunch, and then we went out into the lobby of the hotel.

People recognized Trudeau, and called out his name. They simply said,

"Pierre."

While we sat down on a chair to pull on his boots—it was March, snow was still piled deep in the narrow side streets—three men wearing Stetsons ambled by. One looked in his direction.

"Hey, look, guys, it's Pierre."

The three sidled up, smiling. They jostled one another, approaching directly.

"Pierre! . . . We miss you," one man said.

Trudeau stood up to shake their hands, greeting each in turn.

"You couldn't possibly be from the West." He nodded at their impressive Stetsons.

"But we are!" Another man laughed. "We're here on business from Saskatoon. And I never voted for you."

"Neither did I," the tallest man said.

"I didn't either," the other man admitted.

"No, I never did," the first man who'd spoken said. "We're mostly NDP out there. But, hey, we miss you anyway."

The two others nodded, and they laughed again, and all shook hands once more, and chatted quickly, and said goodbye.

*

I still see in my mind how people waved to him in the street, and hear how people used his first name, calling out in that strangely possessive way.

So we go on reading him, finding out new details in exposed records that challenge our preconceptions, turning the pages of a life backwards and forwards, each person "an infinite, perpetual book" (adapting Sainte-Beuve), and a web of entangling associations. We recognize again how much wisdom it takes to know anything about someone.

And truly he keeps coming through because the books people are writing, the webs we are weaving, the memories we are forming, the images we are storing, include him.

Call it our mythology, and our history. In these pages, and webs, we continue to read, or to direct the cursor towards *search*. In this way we always find ourselves at the beginning.

I remember how people often stopped on the street and said goodbye to him, and now this has become how I say goodbye, a farewell that holds him clearly in my memory and in my imagination where no one and nothing leaves or fades, that Arcadian access. This is where the higher self that sometimes made its way into Trudeau's heart and actions never stops pressing questions in crucial moments and hints of time evolving towards the fulfillments of a just society.

*

Stay an enigma, Pierre. Remain an invocation, in the minds of many. For our sake we should keep the mysteries of identity. Historians and biographers will try to reconcile in you what you would not—and could not—reconcile in yourself. But we should make the unresolved a portion of our understanding of all journeys. By maintaining the mystery we keep something unpredictably alive about ourselves, and keep our longings and intensities sharp and risky.

In the unresolved, our unfolding continues in our imaginations and therefore in our souls, grappling up from bare-bone facts.

Pierre, maybe you knew that if we preserve the elements of mystery, then we will welcome the idea of the stranger, the foreigner, the exile in his own home, the outsider, the rootless immigrant of the imagination, certainly what is (at the very least) beyond the customary. Keep the shadows and the enigmas, and you ask people to hold their wars within, never to fully surface, or to be fully explained. Sufi mystics taught for centuries that this is the truest meaning of jihad: what is to be carried on within, not to be turned into a literal holy war. Thus we head into the currents of mystery, in our en-route hustle along the staggering paths we take or choose, those often obscure ways in our fading pasts and unknowable futures.

There may be only one story, Frye said. It begins when a Sphinx, in whatever appearance, asks, What is human? But the question is cloaked in a fierce riddle that leads to more questions, and more of the quest that may end up being a danger even to one's self. There will be as many versions of this story as there are stars.

People suffer from the absence, or mistrust, of the riddling story, "the wax with many moulds" (Pythagoras). Without it we may fall into cynicism without bottom, or seek a fundamentalism that will seemingly provide a steady foundation. Yet the riddle of identity thrives. The e-cosmos makes it obvious how this story ripples worldwide through images and sensations and impressions and sprawls of data, moving us deeply into universal emotion.

Pierre, you said, "Go beyond the powers that be." Trust this movement in ourselves. That is the most arduous of challenges. Ideas of country, interpretations of motives and events, will come and go. But follow our fascinations, ourselves, and trust this. That must be why in your retirement, your final manifestation was an embodiment of opposition to mandarins and bureaucratic officials, old structures of thought, divisive and prolonged hatreds and grievances, political contrivances and backroom alliances.

You were drawn to hazardous intersections and lines of a complex evolution,

> And I know that there is no
> straight road in this world—
> only a giant labyrinth
> of intersecting crossroads.
>
> And steadily our feet
> keep walking & creating
> —like enormous fans—
> these roads in embryo.
>
> (Lorca)

There is electricity's fire roistering through communication networks.

There is the fire of inspiration, coming from spiritedness.

There is the rose of identity, flowering in ways no one can foresee.

And there is the flowering that is the symbol of watchfulness, so Buddhists teach: the inner eye widening to accept knowledge.

The mind is an upturned cup, waiting to receive. Zen masters instruct their students at the beginning of their training to empty themselves of preconceptions. We could adapt the upturned cup of the *koan* to become the satellite dish and the radioscope receiver. Think of the arrays of electronic bowls scouring the sky like wombs waiting for inseminating waves in the final frames of Roger Zemeckis's film *Contact*.

The flowering and the fires come together in our dreams of ourselves, and those who appear in spectacular intensities. Our e-media increasingly resemble our dreams. It reminds us of light and darkness, and it shows these endlessly streaming now, in the way cosmic dust swirls, among us.

Leaders, celebrities, criminals, cult figures, sports heroes, newscasters, singers, reprobates and saints—we don't know who any of these ethereal figures and types truly are, and yet through satellite beams and links they inhabit our planes and spaces. They are powerfully influential. The worlds of myth move through the tides of images we let loose into our living rooms.

When we engage these energies, and admit them, we add to their invocations. Have we ever fully left the sacred space that is the crossroad of many times and spaces?

We live again with apparitions, and they are speaking. The apparitions and images are back, rebellious mists, deriding the emphases we put on the merely material. Every day, and night, our senses are being massaged, and aroused. We know the signs of this by our perpetual dissatisfaction, and our easy enchantments. In the world amphitheatre we have created by electronic means, these energies re-present themselves, and screens and cells flood us with much more than data.

Pierre, I remember when you quietly said—something you thought so obvious it didn't need to be emphasized—

"Go beyond the powers that be."

I've come to think it's a key. It is what I will remember most vividly from our encounters, now and then: Go beyond.

Pulse in Matter

Go beyond . . . but to what?

I was reading poetry at the library in my town, and talking about Canada and the global media theatre. A frozen white night in deep winter; the cold blast kept people home. But a small group, eager for conversation, came to the hall set aside for talks. Through the glass windows of the room I saw the swimming pool in the fitness centre attached to the library. The pool's light flickered on the walls, like a silver-blue aurora.

A man softly called out in the Q and A period,

"What do you think Trudeau would say about all this?"

The man was referring to the controversy over assigning "a nation within a united Canada" status to Quebec.

It wasn't the first time I'd been asked that question.

What would Trudeau say? What did he say in our conversations that might give us a clue to how he might have responded?

"But what would Trudeau do about so many issues?" a woman asked. She mentioned cynicism and disillusionment, hinting at cancerous distress.

A muttering in the small group, as if others had hoped to ask something similar.

My first answer was to say, look at what he said and did. He went on record about the issues closest to him. We need only look back. I didn't speak for him. We should be careful about thinking that anyone did, or ever could.

Then I gave more consideration to these honest questions and rough anxieties. I could almost hear the group imploring, here we are, in eco-disaster and the communications' hazing, bereft of guidance. Lies, and bigger lies, sometimes saturate the news. No one could be sure where to turn.

They wanted answers—leadership, anything that might help.

My answer was perhaps too abrupt. I kept going back to his statement in one of my last encounters with Trudeau that we should "go beyond the powers that be."

And yet it kept coming to me: Was Trudeau himself, or rather were his ideas, in danger of becoming orthodoxy? He had spent a good deal of his life resisting simplistic answers. He railed against closed borders and insularity. When the higher energy surged through him, he spoke for openness.

Thus what he would say now was no longer the point. He was here in his time to ask questions, to be the wanderer, the rebel and provocateur, the liberal activist, the warrior-guardian, the statesman, the suffering parent and the reclusive elder. These were the parts that he played, or, evocatively, they were the parts that played him.

Surely his response would be to say, turn inward. Ask yourselves what you would do. This is the mystic us. That is the deepest part of the legacy. Where are you? What do you wish to see? What do you want to have happen? Mounier and Teilhard directed him towards the value and the right of personhood, and the energy of the cosmopolitan feeling envelope, the pulse in matter. Trudeau acknowledged in 1971 that in his formative years, these two thinkers, and Kierkegaard, "influenced me most." If we add Kierkegaard to the formations, we re-see at once the idea of "the leap of faith"; the uprooting moment—dream, listen, read the signs, know yourself (even if it means entering spiritual chaos), move your self to be free.

The spirit that once (perhaps briefly) moved him is found in transcendence, justice, ethics and promise. Words tinged with grandeur, they form the core of the questions that we are being asked all the time. We're not merely being asked them—we are, in our moment of summit and abyss, being pounded by them. The word "promise" whispers in our ears, and then, when we stun ourselves into near deafness, the word is shouted. Promise: it is the inkling, the call; it says, look inward, look ahead. Mind, or the Universal Spirit, will find ways through the exigencies in those people willing to undertake quests of learning and knowing, wherever these processes may lead.

Some will pilgrimage. Some will stand still and receive, weaving through the complexities of the signals. Each recognizing this is it; we are at an edge, on cusps of expectation and apocalypse. Enormous pressures are throwing you and me into extreme states of vulnerability. The electrical waves through our light machines, the earth's pollution heating to the point of disaster, the unity of emotions after catastrophes, the borderless disorder which is the new order, the emanations of each beating heart, all this we know. We know.

"Promise" is another tributary word with streams of ambiguity. It means a gift, an honouring, a seal, a pledge, an avowal, a vocation, an engagement. A rainbow is a broken circle—a portion of beauty—that presses us with promise. The other half of the circle, the destination of the bridge of mists, is in us.

The word "promise" means to send forth, to send out. It has links with "mission," and even "missile." *"The woods are lovely, dark and deep/But I have promises to keep/And miles to go before I sleep/And miles to go before I sleep."* This stanza from Robert Frost's "Stopping by Woods on a Snowy Evening," which places the pilgrim at a crossroads "between the woods and frozen lake," were lines that Trudeau knew by heart. He uttered them on the occasion of his third electoral victory in 1980. To whom was he making the promise? . . . To the people who'd elected him? . . . To his party, to whom he owed favours? . . . To the moments ahead? . . . To the Charter of Rights that was soon to come? . . . To himself? . . . To the destiny he had always followed? Perpetually unfinished quests; these are part of the legacy, too.

Trudeau could be the ruthless arbiter. The examples from his career are legion. He pragmatically experimented with ideas and forms, dealing with the practical issues of governance, reacting in the way politicians do, effectively or ineffectively, to whatever local or global problems struck. The reactive sides of politics are called "fire-fighting" by those in the trade. The mystic compass of his inwardness kept all this (more or less) intelligible to him. He knew the game of politics, and was willing to use the people around him to fulfill the details of his highly specific agenda: to realize the country of many voices.

If we want to know what he would say, it is easy to find in his words his original protest against orthodoxy. Here is what he wrote in 1967,

> There are no absolute truths in politics. The best ideologies, having arisen at specific times to combat given abuses, become the worst if they survive the needs which gave them birth. Through history all great reformers were sooner or later betrayed by the excessive fidelity of their disciples. When a reform starts to be universally popular, it is more than likely that is has already become reactionary, and free men must then oppose it.

Trudeau often wrote and spoke vehemently. Sometimes his voice carried alarming autocratic intonations. This was part of his style. But we shouldn't mistake his impassioned conviction for any absolute insight into truth. He spoke for himself. Everything else was the journey each of us must make, in our own way.

In 1962, in his essay "New Treason of the Intellectuals," he quoted Renan, "'Man is bound neither to his language nor to his race; he is bound only to himself because he is a free agent, or in other words a moral being.'"

A just society is a point ahead of us. It is greater than anyone. This is no doubt why we cannot find where Trudeau himself found it. Incompletion and evasiveness leave us with "creative tide" and "increasing powers of self-determination" (Teilhard de Chardin). Even a nation is provisional. We should recall, we create our borders, and Trudeau, in his actions, kept crossing his, with sometimes wounding consequences in his private life. But this is what the process will bring if one trusts in going beyond.

A wound is also a signature of the opening.

Words are openings, so are images, and symbols.

The pulse of his spirit is in words and in images that have become iconic.

We see this in the two vivid and contrary pictures from 1977 and 1968. In his pirouette behind the Queen we were informed, go your own way. In the warrior fury that came over him when he sat still during the St. Jean Baptiste Day riot, we were given a warning. The prophetic dimension of the image was the coming of War Measures. The warning was to anyone who used terrorist violence in the name of revolution: this will not be allowed to happen here.

These images are signs, and signals. One is a taunt, the other is severe. One was choreographed, the other was a response. They ask (again), what path will you choose?

*

"In crisis their souls are visible," Anne Carson said, when writing of the characters in Euripides' tragedies. (In homage to Carson, I've adapted her line through my reflections.) The heroic players were substitutes in the ritual dramas written, in all likelihood, between 455 and 400 BC; they stood in for the terrors and griefs we feel. This is catharsis, the release of emotion through art. In the global mystery amphitheatre, and in the interactive zones we call (with sublime irony) our terminals, we are the actors and the audience. But there is no cathartic relief on media earth from the ache of its emotions. Our entire space and time communicates, our senses overstimulated by sound, vision, scent, taste, touch. In these immersions comes the mythic story ("Who?") in vast telepathic patterns. The planet's beat is so inescapably loud it keeps all of us awake.

McLuhan said that most people know the present only through a rearview mirror. We look backwards, like travellers on a train, trying to settle into our daydreams and newspapers, our iPods and snacks, faces almost relaxing into relief, sitting firmly with our backs to the future, and its inevitable rush towards us. When I summoned Trudeau I looked again to his past, and to mine. But he was more interested in turning the mirror forward, to catch the glimmer of what was coming here, now.

> Not fare well,
> But fare forward
> (T.S. Eliot)

We hear the cosmopolis heart, and know the cries of all visible souls. The heart often resembles a rose when vividly rendered in iconography. The electricity that pumps through wires and over the wireless space, and the energy that beats through arteries and on nerve-ends, burns when heated by new intensities, and by new breath.

The world blazes openly. What would happen if we stood up, fully present, on fire in ourselves, and turned to face it?

The man at the library on that winter night had asked the invaluable question. The woman's follow-up was essential too. They offered, in their unexpected way, pivotal moments. I'm indebted to them, and have responded here.

*

Sometimes the higher self comes upon us, and we speak of justice, or of love, truly. We may feel first principles, and then speak of a Universal Charter that addresses opportunity, the right to participate, the right to develop a personality, a common origin, the dynamism of energies that enlighten but don't impose. Then the higher self leaves, and we are left wrecked, or receptive, perhaps confused, perhaps wiser—nevertheless remembering—and we go on, day by day, doing what we must, one side of ourselves waiting for the opening to come again.

Notes and Acknowledgments

In December 2006 I stayed overnight in the Robert ("Bob") Rae Room in Building II of Massey College, on the campus of the University of Toronto. I was told by John Fraser, the genial Master, that the bed in the room was Trudeau's. He often slept there when he visited the city, to see his daughter, Sarah.

The college room had a small fireplace, a desk, a couch, two chairs and a small library. I found the bed narrow, and hard. It was a monastic cot. Which means it was uncomfortable. I knew I would sleep lightly in that cold room.

Students and guests alike had been locked into the small campus grounds by the warden. Silence and stillness soon settled in over the college.

Contemplative, after the evening's event, I looked for something to read. I thumbed my way through the books on the shelves. Near the bed I found *American Sphinx: the Character of Thomas Jefferson*, by Joseph J. Ellis. It had been published in a paperback Vintage edition in 1998. The title was enticing. I started reading slowly.

It came to me that what Ellis said about the enigmatic Jefferson echoed the thoughts and observations people often had about Trudeau. Ellis began his book with reflections on Jefferson's "contradictions and inconsistencies," "his capacity to play hide and seek with himself." He evoked how Jefferson was "endlessly elusive and extraordinarily adroit at covering his tracks." I read of the protean Jefferson, his "accessible mysteriousness." It was Jefferson who gave the Constitution of the United States its personal spiritual slant, and its republican yearning—a longing frustrated, I noted, by the imperial power that American had become. Jefferson was quoted saying the promise of the new comes when "all eyes are opened or are opening to the rights of men."

I saw similarities in these essential dreamers. And I saw contrasts. Trudeau was an advocate of a form of government that was neither minimalist nor non-interventionist. Government had a role in shaping and providing structures for people. They shared skepticism about unbridled executive power, however. Mercurial and receptive, they were both highly sensitive, with deep needs for reclusive time. Both were uneasy with orthodoxies. When they intervened in political turning points, they did so with energy and provocative stances in writing and public demonstration. They cultivated audacities that kept each a stranger to even those who loved them.

I had the thought, sudden, sharp, that perhaps Trudeau

himself read this book when he stayed there. The title would have appealed to him. He was intrigued by Jefferson, so I knew from our conversations. I could see synchronicities: the framer of our Constitution would have looked attentively at the man who had written the American Constitution. Trudeau was fascinated by patterns that showed similar longings for a just society elsewhere. He would have been attracted to knowing what was best in our neighbours, and what we shared with them, in this mythic space, full of possessions and presences.

It was an eerie moment, while I read, and sat in the college room.

The book became one that I would incorporate into portions of my reflections.

*

I've been writing about Trudeau in one way or another for twenty years. I still haven't come to a final assessment of him, and I think it unlikely that I ever will. It's been part of my education in life to write about him. Here again he has provided me with opportunities to think through and express ideas.

Many authors and images have made major contributions to this book. I've read others' books about him, and often admired them. And I've watched CBC docudramas that always seemed to faithfully capture a part of him, but never the whole person.

I have to list the ones who have helped or guided me. John English, especially, for confirming details, and providing quotations, in his admirable *Citizen of the World: The Life of Pierre Elliott Trudeau, Volume One: 1919–1968*. He also graciously helped to illuminate details through letters and conversations. Monique and Max Nemni (friends who made major contributions to the Trudeau Era Conference in 1998) provided fresh and disturbing details in the first volume of their biographical exploration. Others include Christina McCall and Stephen Clarkson, Richard Gwyn, George Radwanski, Ron Graham, Teri McLuhan, Nancy Southam, Tom Axworthy, Jim Coutts, Andrew Cohen, Jack Granatstein, Lawrence Martin, Claude Coutere, Guy Laforest, Kenneth McRoberts, Karen Alliston, Rick Archbold, Jennifer Glossop, Alison Maclean, Ivon Owen, through *Trudeau Albums*; and Robert Denham, for the Frye *Notebooks*.

I'm indebted to James Hillman's books for an alternative reading of the role of psyche.

Stephen Clarkson said, "He taunts us still" during the keynote address he gave at the Trudeau Era conference at York University in 1998.

*

Theologians may quarrel with what must appear a murky disregard of the distinctions between mystic, metaphysical, spiritual, religious, Gnostic, transcendence, immanence. These slippery words point to experiences beyond language.

I'm aware that the terms probably shouldn't be used interchangeably. I've left them resonating, nevertheless, like vibrating notes, like multiple entry points, to nurture their ambivalences and ambiguities. Watch the lexical auras that cluster around them, and you'll find that the words we use to probe the sacred remain limited. This is revealing in itself. It is no doubt why theologians quarrel so intently over them.

*

Sources include Gail Godwin, Anne Carson, Simone Weil's *Gravity and Grace*, translated by Emma Crawford and Mario von der Ruhr, Joseph Campbell, David Rosenberg's translation of the *Book of J*, Caroline Weber, Dr. Vivian S. Rambihar and his writings. The quotations and revisions from Teilhard de Chardin and Emmanuel Mounier are taken from the standard translations of their works. The Pascal quotes and paraphrases were culled from the Penguin Classics translation by A.J. Krailsheimer.

I am aware of how this translation often differs from others. My debt is enormous to the *Portable Emerson*, edited by Carl Bode; it's been a bottomless resource. The selections of quotations from Marcus Aurelius's *Meditations* are from the "New Translation" by Gregory Hays. Most of the fragments I found in Books X and XI. I owe a special debt to the McLuhan family, and particularly Mrs. Corinne McLuhan, for permission to quote from Marshall McLuhan's *The Book of Probes*, published in 2003, by Gingko Press.

Some parts of this book were published in radically different forms. The essays and articles provided springboards for further forays. Most of the original passages barely exist now, in the transformations that took place while I was writing this through. Still, it's a good idea to acknowledge where the pieces first appeared.

"Taciturn Mask, Elusive I" was published under the title "The Lion in Winter." It was the final chapter of *Trudeau's Shadow: The Life and Legacy of Pierre Elliott Trudeau*, edited by Andrew Cohen and J.L. Granatstein, and published by Random House of Canada, in Toronto, in 1998.

"Eulogy" was adapted from my piece "We're on Our Own Now," published in "The Legacy" section of *The Globe and Mail*, on September 30, 2000. It is the only piece here that is close to being an intact version of the first publication.

"We Are the Images" is an amplification and extension of "A Canadian Icon," published in the *Ottawa Citizen*, December 31, 2000. The chapter bears little resemblance to the newspaper version.

"North of the Future" is also a free adaptation and amplification of the editorial I wrote, titled, inexplicably by the editors, "Waiting for Trudeau," in *The Globe and Mail*, on November 21, 2000.

A large part of the material on the abolition of the monarchy was orally presented in June 2001, at Moses Znaimer's IdeaCity in Toronto.

"Inward Pressure" was first presented at the conference "The Hidden Pierre Elliott Trudeau" at St. Jerome's College at the University of Waterloo in 2002. My presentation was later broadcast on TVO's *Big Ideas*. An essay version, quite different, was printed under the title "Soul's Flow" in *The Hidden Pierre Elliott Trudeau: The Faith Behind the Politics*, edited by John English, Richard Gwyn and P. Whitney Lackenbauer, published by Novalis, in Toronto, in 2004.

A small section of "Turning" appeared in *Pierre*, edited by Nancy Southam, published by McClelland & Stewart, in Toronto, in 2005.

Many people were part of the processes of this book. They commented, offered suggestions, made recommendations, added observations, questioned what I said, offered more inspirations.

Above all, I'm grateful to my editor, Patrick Crean, at Thomas Allen. He is one of the last editors in the great Max Perkins tradition. I'm also indebted to Janice Zawerbny and Lisa Zaritzky, Wendy Thomas, and Jim Allen and all the team who devote themselves to the production of their books.

I must say thank you to Michael Levine, my agent, and his able assistant, Maxine Quigley. They have been more than mediators over the years. They have been supportive friends. I'm grateful for their goodwill.

My father, Bruce Allen Powe, made comments, sometimes challenging, and helped to strengthen my thoughts during our conversations. I'm indebted to Val Ross, Fulvio Caccia (for many ideas that brought on counterideas), Dorothy and Keith Davey, John Roberts, Professor Andy Tomcik, Professor David Shugarman, Professor Michael Copeland, and John Fraser, my many friends at Trent University who listened to a first airing of the ideas in this work. Also Dennis Mills, who gave me access to many things. My thanks to Valerie Ann Stride; she knew about Trudeau primarily through what she'd seen in images and read in history texts. This book is in part, in its way, a word of explanation.

I'm indebted to Professor Lorraine Eisenstat Weinrib of the University of Toronto, and to Mary Eberts. Both took the time to guide me through the constitutional and legal ramifications of the Supreme Court judgment and of the proposal to abolish the monarchy. Quite charmingly, at the time, both agreed, "The abolition should have been done a long time ago." My argument is based on their conversations and their often detailed explanations.

A special note of thanks goes to my translator and long-time friend, Michelle Tisseyre. I also owe her thanks for the inspired refinement of titles and lines.

I owe much to Friederike Bental and to Carolyn McDermott, who provided invaluable support and mentoring through all my writings and reflections. Deepest thanks to Tania, Sam, Julia, Maria and Kristine, my teachers in Stouffville. And also to Charlene Jones, who helped to crystallize essential thoughts and feelings.

Sean Smith of the Clara Thomas Archives at York University kindly helped me sort through my papers, deposited there, to find the notes I'd stored away. He eagerly went back and forth to the deposits, looking for letters and pages, and did so with good-humoured interest.

The librarians at the Stouffville Public Library have helped me by reserving and ordering books. Catherine Sword handled my barrage of requests with friendly amusement. I also owe a debt to innumerable friends and acquaintances, colleagues and associates, who often indirectly shared a word, a memory, a phrase, an image, a thought, a reaction, a story.

Once more I express my debt to my students in the Department of English at York University. They continue to offer me many opportunities for learning. My thanks to Dr. Robert Drummond, Dean of Arts; his office provided the research grants and the sabbatical leave. Thanks also to Professor Eric Willis, former Master of Stong College, for his firm support over the years; and to Professor Kim Michasiw for his, too. The Ontario Arts Council has provided financial backing over the years; and for this I offer my gratitude.

And last, to my children, Katie and Thomas, who were with me on many occasions when Trudeau became part of my life again. They've in their own way grown up in the shadow of his complex aspirations.

— BWP

Challenge Words:

Sacagawea
Lewis
buffalo
Native American
snow
Meriwether
William
boat
where

Meriwether Lewis was a brave man. He liked to hunt.

Lewis had a job to explore some land in the West.

Lewis needed help on his trip west.

Lewis had a good pal named William Clark.

Clark went with Lewis and some other men, and they left on the trip west.

First, they went on a boat made of wood.

They fished for food.

Then they walked in the woods.

As they went, they saw elk, foxes, and birds.

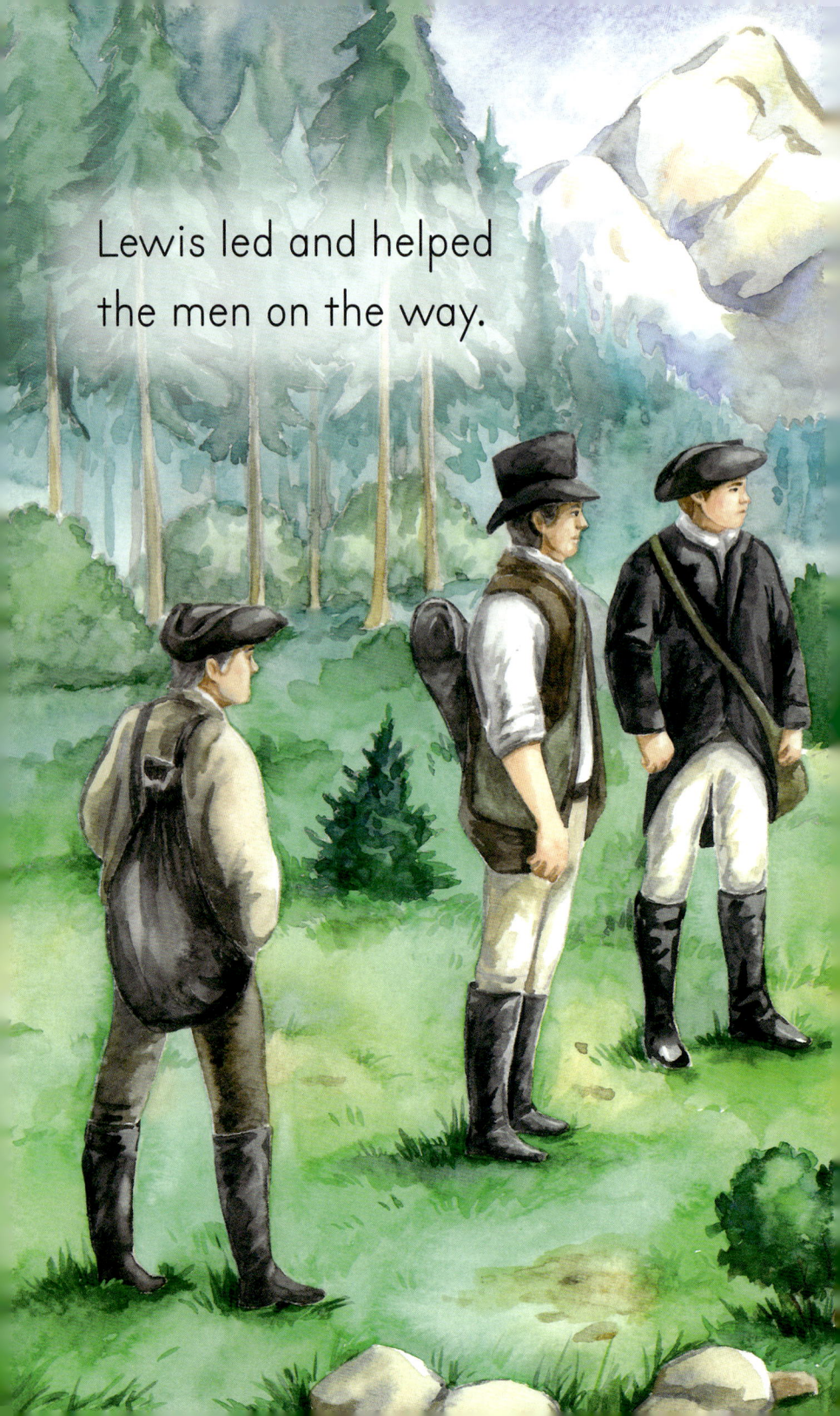

He hunted for food with his men.

Lewis made notes of things he saw.

Clark took notes too.

He even made maps of where they went.

One day, Lewis and Clark saw many buffalo eating grass.

Lewis and Clark went a long way, but then it started to snow.

It was getting too cold.

They made a fort to keep out of the snow.

They met some Native Americans who lived close to them.

One of them was a girl named Sacagawea.

When the snow was gone, Lewis and Clark had to go west.

They still had to find a path to the sea.

Sacagawea went with them on the trip.

They met more Native American tribes as they went.

Lewis and Clark traded with the tribes for horses and food.

Sacagawea had a baby boy.

She took him on her back as they went.

They called him Pomp.

They went over tall hills filled with pine trees.

At last, they made it to the sea.

They were so happy!

They saw the sand and the waves.

They planted an American flag in the ground and made another fort.

They learned a lot about the sea.

They took the things they had found and the maps they had made.

Lewis and Clark and the Native Americans they met helped us learn so much about the West.

More Books from The Good and the Beautiful Library

Ollie the Ox and Other Animal Tales
by Kathy Leckrone and Shannen Yauger

Brent's Bot
by Tessa Greene

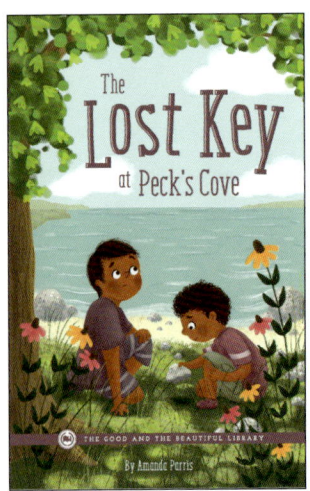

The Lost Key at Peck's Cove
by Amanda Parris

Prince Percy and the Big Red Ruby
by Jenny Phillips

goodandbeautiful.com